Diamond Discoveries of a Woman Preacher

To Bill B

Blessings! Thanks
for your
encouragement —

Cozetta R Garrett

2018

Diamond Discoveries of a Woman Preacher

*A Word for Female Clergy and Those
Wanting to Understand Them*

Cozette R. Garrett

FOREWORD BY
G. Lee Ramsey Jr.

RESOURCE *Publications* · Eugene, Oregon

DIAMOND DISCOVERIES OF A WOMAN PREACHER
A Word for Female Clergy and Those Wanting to Understand Them

Resource Publications
An Imprint of Wipf and Stock Publishers
199 W. 8th Ave., Suite 3
Eugene, OR 97401

www.wipfandstock.com

PAPERBACK ISBN: 978-1-4982-9826-1
HARDCOVER ISBN: 978-1-4982-4876-1
EBOOK ISBN: 978-1-4982-9827-8

Manufactured in the U.S.A.

I dedicate this book to:

Irma Beard Rogers, *My Mother*
Linnie Mae Wallace Garrett, *My Mother-in-Law*
Rev. Dr. Carolyn Knight, *The first Woman Preacher I heard*
Pastor Lois Moore Williams, *My first Woman Preacher Mentor*

Contents

Foreword

MOST OF US HAVE heard the phrase "a diamond in the rough."
It signifies that something of great value is hidden within an ap-
parently worthless exterior. A hard, crusty layer of outer rock
obscures a shining stone that is trapped deeply within, waiting
to be discovered, polished, and released to brilliantly shine. In
Christian ministry, too often that hidden dimension of Christian
leadership has been the lives of faithful women. Women who God
has called to serve equally among men as preachers, pastors, worship leaders, educators, chaplains, and administrators, but whose
God given call to ministry the church and society has been slow
to acknowledge. Even now in the early twenty-first century, following decades of progress in civil rights and the empowerment of
women and other minorities, in many Christian quarters women's
call to official ministry is too frequently suppressed, ignored, or
denied. Their gifts remain obscured, their voices stifled. But help is
on the way. In this sparkling book, Cozette R. Garrett has released
the diamond in the rough.

Here in *Diamond Discoveries of a Woman Preacher,* you will
first discover the voice of a true gem of a person. Cozette Garrett's loving, gentle, yet clear and defining voice shines through on
every page I know because it was my privilege to work alongside
her for seven years in Memphis Theological Seminary's Sustaining
Pastoral Excellence project. She is not only a remarkable preacher
and leader but a person of authentic faith. And her smile, if you
could see it, would dance right off the page and into the discour-
aged places of your own heart. Whether you have ever met Cozette
Garrett or not, you only need to read the first page to know that

you are listening to the words of someone who knows how to be a true companion, a compassionate friend. And what she wants to do here is nothing more and nothing less than share with us, her readers, as friend to friend, what she has learned and lived as a woman preacher.

You will also discover in the substance of the book precious stones of wisdom about Christian ministry. Yes, Dr. Garrett crafts these gentle words of wisdom first for other women in ministry, female laypersons, or women who are seeking clarity about how best to love God and neighbor as a Christian believer. But the men should also listen well, for Cozette's vision and experience offers compelling direction for how women and men can move forward *together* in ministry as we serve the same Lord within the rich diversity of the Body of Christ. We need to hear her voice and learn from her mindfulness in Christian ministry.

Light shines in many directions from the treasures that Dr. Garrett unearths in this succinct book. Her hard-won wisdom regarding women in ministry is distilled from over twenty-five years of service within congregations, hospitals, seminaries, and faith-based community ministries. She has been surrounded by supportive family, friends, and mentors. Out of all this, she offers sage advice about how to both serve God in ordained ministry and to maintain balance in life. She reminds us of the importance of sharing the load of Christian ministry with others. And she speaks frankly about sexuality and ministry. These and many other precious stones of ministry she holds out to us, carefully cut and polished for our edification.

Like the pearl of great price, *Diamonds Discoveries of a Woman Preacher,* is waiting to be found by each of us. You have in your hands a rich discovery, not of perishing earthly value but filled instead with the "immeasurable riches" of the grace of God (Ephesians 2:7, NRSV). So go ahead. Dig-in. Crack open the cover. See what treasures you will find.

G. Lee Ramsey Jr.
Memphis Theological Seminary

Words of Thanks

I THANK GOD FOR allowing me to write the words in this book and to recall stories from my personal life and ministry. Thanks go to so many people who helped me to live my life and to give service. With support and trust from others, I was able to minister to the larger Memphis community and also to congregations in the surrounding area. Because of my extensive hours spent serving others, my family sacrificed so much. I give special thanks to my husband, Solomon M. Garrett Jr., and to our daughters, Dana D. Garrett and Marloe D.G. Mackie, who are now adults. As I ministered to people I listened to so many stories—some of which are recorded in these pages without names or other identifying information. My parents, Willie Robert "Bob" Rogers and Irma Beard Rogers, who are both sleeping in the arms of Our God, sacrificed repeatedly to send me to schools—public and private. I can write today because of their wisdom and support.

I have friends to whom I am deeply indebted for without their listening ears, laughs and encouragement; I could not have endured and enjoyed over 25 years of licensed and ordained ministry to the church and para-church organizations. These personal angels are Lois D. Madison, Carolyn Dukes Newby Tisdale, Nettie Tipton, Ursula Welters Elliot, Francis Joiner, Josephine "Jo" Weaver, Florence "Flo" Roach, and Louise Harris. Special thanks are also given to *significant mentors* in *Chapter 5* of this book entitled "Dare To Mine the Minds Where the Lord Directs".

Several God-daughters and sons inspired me and gave me fresh humor and wisdom as I listened to their stories while they grew to be fine women and men of today and tomorrow. They are Davitria Harrell, Terry Lynn "Tinker" Newby Mearidy, Navy Commander Edward Newby, Karen Newby, and Angela Harris.

I praise God for three male colleagues and advisors who, ironically, all went to be with the Lord in 2012. Even though it was not always acceptable for men in some circles to encourage female clergy, Dr. David L. Boyle, Rev. T.O. Crivens and Minister David N. Flagg supported me and my ministry in numerous ways. Their wives—Linda, Ulanda, and Dolores were and are my personal treasures.

For the initial readers of my first draft of this book, I sincerely thank Dr. G. Lee Ramsey and Rev. Sonia L. Walker for their honest consultation, friendship, and encouragement. I thank God for my son-in-love Charlie W. Mackie, my friends—Cindy Vaughn and Lisa M. Vasser, and for those clergypersons like Rev. Gail Gaddie, Rev. Lenn Milam, Rev. Delesslyn Kennebrew, Dr. Rosalyn R. Nichols, Rev. Virzola Law, Dr. Allen Wesley, Rev. Lillie Matlock, and Dr. Jean Johnson who individually became a part of a collective voice that pressed me to write and record my thoughts. I am particularly grateful to them for their tenacity and persistence in keeping me accountable as I continued to write while doing ministry. My sister and brother, Rev. Delphine Rogers Newsum and Rev. W. Robert Rogers Jr. have known the joys and challenges of doing ministry. I thank them for sharing my loads by loving me and sharing stories.

Thanks go to all the church families who allowed me and are still allowing me to practice, learn, grow and serve the women, men and children of their faith communities. Special thanksgiving to Memphis, Tennessee churches—Mississippi Boulevard Christian Church (Disciples of Christ), Community of Faith Christian Church (Disciples of Christ), Macedonia Baptist Church, Olivet Baptist Church (now New Olivet), Central Baptist Church, Grace United Methodist Church, and my childhood congregation—First Baptist Church of Brownsville, Tennessee. And to the Memphis Theological Seminary staff and faculty, I say thank you for helping me to broaden my knowledge base to include women who dare to call themselves *preachers*.

Cozette R. Garrett

Spring 2016
Memphis, Tennessee

Introduction

At first, I found it extremely difficult—or downright hard—to believe in the possibility of there being women preachers! Even though I am female, I could not conceive the thought without feeling tension and anxiety. Having been reared among National Baptists, Catholics, and Church of God in Christ faithful and loving members, there was no room for those women who had the title *preacher*. Certainly there were so-called mothers of the church, evangelists, healers, and nuns but no female priests or preachers were ordained and set apart for those public ministries.

Women comprised a majority number in all congregations with whom I had been associated but their leadership roles were predominantly supportive. The long volunteer hours and the amount of donated money often exceeded the males in the church or parish community. Clergy leadership surely recognized the contributions of women. My family was one which had women who were the backbone of church families in several denominations. However, their services were not given as ordained clergy.

On the other hand, I came from a family of men who had faithfully dedicated themselves to lifetimes of working in, around and about church and para-church communities. My extended family was sprinkled, sprayed and infused with male clergy and male lay persons who were committed to living out their callings and gifts. I am proud of their service. I am disappointed, however, that women were not *initially* encouraged to live out their calling as preachers.

I am very pleased and grateful that my family *did* fervently believe in training and supporting female leaders who could excel

INTRODUCTION

in business, education, and community circles. Generally, the value of church work and leadership roles for women *and* men were emphatically encouraged and supported. However, there was one exception. The concept of women serving as clergy was basically ignored. Women were *not* abused or verbally upbraided. They were appreciated, as a whole, but female clergypersons were simply not discussed or promoted. This fact was a part of my formation that I did not consciously address until my late thirties!

In 1982, I was a member of Olivet Baptist Church where the pastor was Rev. Kenneth T. Whalum Sr. Even though it was an unpopular stance in many denominations, the now late Rev. Whalum firmly believed in the existence, ministry, and ordination of women preachers. At that time, I was silent but adamantly against his belief! With the exception of his stance on female clergy, I embraced Rev. Whalum's theology, philosophy, and focus toward church empowerment and reformation. Based on his conviction, he invited Rev. Dr. Carolyn Knight to be our Women's Day Speaker. Even though I had heard she was a dynamic preacher, I was literally shocked and appalled by his invitation and thought that he was making a mistake in bringing her to preach. Because I respected my pastor and was a dutiful choir member, I had intended to sing and then to discreetly leave the church premises prior to the sermon. On the above Women's Day, I believe that Divine Intervention took place.

Olivet's Women's Days were always packed to capacity with members and special-day-in-the-Black-church attendees. And since Rev. Knight was the first ordained female clergy to preach at Olivet, there was an even larger crowd who attended the worship for this special day. When I finished singing, there was no apparent, easy exit! I was forced to remain in the choir, seated directly behind the powerful, wonderful, preaching woman-of-God. She was absolutely superior in presentation and obviously anointed by God to do the work of preacher.

As she preached, tears rolled down my face and I heard the words of the prophet in Isaiah 6: 5 saying, "Woe is me! for I am undone; because I am a man of unclean lips . . . " (KJV) And I

heard my own words echo within me, "Woe is me! for I am undone; because I am a *woman* of unclean lips . . . " I did not yet
know or accept that I was female clergy but I certainly knew, from
that day forward, that *women clergy were indeed real and set apart*
to give their service as a mouthpiece for Our God. I am eternally
grateful for Dr. Knight's faithfulness and for Rev. Whalum's coura-
geous foresight. These were pivotal preliminary steps that I had to
take toward accepting my calling to preach.

While my family supported and valued church leadership
and service by both genders, it was not until the late 1980s that
they began to embrace the reality of female clergy. In 1984, I accepted my calling as minister and then I began my personal journey to become licensed and later ordained in 1992. It was a relief
and release of energy that has continued to unfold, blossom and
explode. God has blessed me to serve as a chaplain—hospital and
hospice, a community & congregational organizer, a senior pastor,
a seminary teacher, and program director who supported clergy
and their families as they gave Christian service.

The journey has been a good and fruitful one but often personally exhausting and confusing. In the early days, I mistakenly
surmised that I did not know how to be a woman preacher. My
mentors and role models were not obviously apparent to me. Even
though I had previously served as a state training coordinator at
the Department of Human Services in Memphis and a program
coordinator at three organizations, I was unsure of this new clergy
leadership role. I did not see or dare to claim that the above past
work experiences *plus* my development as a mother and wife were
more than adequate initial training for ordained ministry. It was
not clear to me that the many hours I had spent in church and
community volunteerism were seminary *class pre-requisites* that
were foundational for my becoming an ordained minister. It took
me years to discern that all of the children and youth plays that
God had allowed me to direct with the assistance of hundreds of
parents and volunteers had been holy preparation designed to
ready me for a life as ordained clergy. Additionally, my undergraduate degree focused in journalism and speech & drama education

were perfect training for the clergy opportunities that were about to emerge in my life story. God was kind, gentle, wise, and patient enough to orchestrate a *specialized training program* so that my diamond-in-the-rough state could shine forth one day.

At 38 years old, I went to Memphis Theological Seminary, cautiously taking one class at a time! I entered a new life with fresh colleagues in ministry—women and men who helped me to open doors to a newly found space. Often I felt as if I had crawled into or stumbled upon a spiritual or mental diamond mine with newly discovered gems and gifts that I have now continued to use and unwrap over the last 25 or more years! I wish somebody had written a book or two to help me to know how to mine, search for, discover, and polish the diamonds that were already in my life. While I believe that the material written in these pages can be certainly relevant and applicable to all new clergypersons, this book is especially dedicated to those women who are in search of gemstones that will sparkle and point the way to greater clarity in finding the path to becoming a *woman preacher*.

There are many names that women are called if they are clergy. Whether licensed or ordained, some people will call us minister, prophetess, evangelist, chaplain, messenger, speaker, doctor, missionary or clergy but then choose to never say *preacher*—one who is called to deliver public messages from God Almighty. There are other churched and unchurched people, who will withhold the title pastor and believe that women are unworthy of leading congregations, performing liturgical worship, and administering sacraments to faith communities. Some people prefer that we dress differently so that we look more like men or appear very modest. Sometimes parishioners seem to feel more comfortable if female clergypersons look more like the biblical stereotypes and present day male leaders that they revere and love. Considering all of the above, I choose to embrace my femininity and calling to be ordained clergy by choosing to call myself *Woman Preacher*. As you read, I invite you to embrace or substitute the terminology that allows you to experience the authority that God has granted women to preach and lead God's people.

There may be those who will read this book who do not believe that there is a unique—often hidden—layer of truth to being female clergy. This material is also intended to bring awareness and greater understanding to the extra facets of being female and clergy. My prayer is that female clergy, their families, and colleagues will be made aware and more sensitive to the ways that we can support each other in our journeys to becoming even more brilliant in God's eyes.

1

Diamonds Come in Different
Shapes and Sizes

THE CHRISTIAN CHURCH UNIVERSAL has difficulty believing that
God calls clergy to serve in other than the local parish. Parish pastoral ministry is certainly an important and critical calling that
should be valued and supported by all congregations and communities. What would we do without the faithful local church pastor who baptizes babies and adults, spends long nights in hospital
family rooms, plans funeral services, and conducts bereavement
aftercare that can continue for years following the committal and
internment? Where would our faith communities be without
clergy who have spent many nights preparing sermons and plead-
ing the cases of teens that have gotten off-track and lost their ways
home? Pastors deserve our greatest respect. To fulfill the work of a
parish pastor is both a great honor and burden. Many clergy families, including spouses and children, have sacrificed their family
time and resources alongside parish pastors who struggled to do
the work of ministry. The world needs the service given by local
church pastors and their families. Even after working several years
to distribute welfare and Medicaid benefits and listening to the
pain of social workers and clients, there was no work that I did at
the Department of Human Services which was more challenging
than that of serving as a senior pastor in a small congregation.

However that being said, local church pastors comprise only a
portion of the clergy who are called to minister to the household of
faith. People needing clergy leaders find themselves in jails, hospital rooms, on battle fields, and military bases. Scared parishioners
who are transferred to new jobs can find hope as they are given

time to talk to workplace counselors or clergypersons who serve in employee assistance programs. Clergy helping hands can be found holding the trembling hands of people and families who are in hospice or going through the tragedies and crises experienced in trauma centers, counseling centers, fraternal organizations, and community para-church ministries that are too numerous and varied to name. Wherever clergypersons serve, it becomes holy ground when God is present and holy rituals are performed for the good of people. The Kingdom of God on earth is not limited to a place of worship built by people. Steeples arise in places where people need access to a visible and viable connection to God.

Ordained priests and preachers bring God to a situation or circumstance because their lives are set apart and consecrated to do the work of the Kingdom. It is hurtful to observe that, all too often, people do not consider the work of clergy as valid or authentic unless the clergypersons are called to serve in the local church body context. When I served in a *more than* full-time position as a licensed minister at a large local church congregation, I visited the hospital where three family members were about to be taken to surgery after a traumatic car accident. Before I was able to reach the hospital, one of the family members had already died during emergency surgery. Intense ministry started as I walked in the hospital family room and continued for several hours. I have learned over the years to ignore some of the things that people say when in panic. It was still painful and insulting for a family member to exclaim, "Thanks so much for coming and praying with us. This is such a serious time. I was devastated and scared. I feel so much better now. You said all the right things. I don't know what we would have done without you . . . I had just hoped that they would send a 'real pastor' in this situation." It took me years to get over and to forgive this statement. Even though the senior pastor and congregation recognized and affirmed my gifts and skills and had officially dispatched me to this assignment, this family member did not fully recognize or appreciate my credentials and dedicated service given in the middle of the night.

Ministers who are serving in and out of the pulpit are *real pastors*. Clergypersons who bring the Eternal One to the faithful in the form of art, music, drama, exercise classes for all ages, and liturgy in all settings—including nursing homes and rehabilitation centers—are *real pastors*. Diamonds shine wherever they are placed so that light can reflect from their surfaces.

What does all of the above have to do with women preachers? Much! Many people can feel justified as they devalue, demean, diminish, and dismiss the validity of female clergy because the woman-in-question has not been called to be a local church senior pastor. *God's intentional design* for some ministers—women and men—is that they live out their faith walks as other than the work of senior pastor. We must also recall that often judicatories, church members, and colleagues will not accept or invite women to serve as senior pastors—even when the female's gifts, training and leadership abilities appear to be well suited for the work. *Congregations and communities must realize and teach that senior pastors do their best work and are healthiest when they do not serve in isolation.* They need the associate pastors, ministers, and other commissioned clergy who serve alongside him or her with God's help. Clergypersons can serve in cooperation and harmony as the Lord permits and assigns work areas.

Traditionally, a church's belief systems are based on reading, studying, and interpreting the scriptures. Often people in our present society do not read the bible personally but depend upon clergy to interpret for us. Unfortunately, when pastoral staff persons are re-telling bible stories and recounting sermon illustrations, the ministry of women has been often minimized or ignored. Because women are serving in capacities other than senior pastors, frequently they are not the ones who are telling the stories to congregations. When the church withholds some respect for and devotion to particular clergypersons, it not only causes the public to withdraw their support for women but it sometimes causes female clergy themselves to doubt their own calling and to hold back as they give service. *Each calling is real and valid if God made the invitation.* My discovery is that each diamond is unique

in color, luster, and fluorescence. God gives the beauty and place-
ment. There is no need to discard any gems. We can use and enjoy
all gifts as God pleases.

> . . . and we sat down to speak to some who had gathered
> there. One of them was Lydia from Thyatira, a merchant
> of expensive purple cloth, who worshiped God. As she lis-
> tened to us, the Lord opened her heart, and she accepted
> what Paul was saying. She was baptized along with other
> members of her household, and she asked us to be her
> guests. "If you agree that I am a true believer in the Lord,"
> she said, "come and stay at my home." And she urged us
> until we agreed.
>
> Acts 16: 13b-15 NLT

> There are different kinds of spiritual gifts, but the same
> Spirit is the source of them all. There are different kinds of
> service, but we serve the same Lord . . . A spiritual gift is
> given to each of us so we can help each other. The human
> body has many parts, but the many parts make up one
> whole body. . . . But our bodies have many parts, and God
> has put each part just where he wants it.
>
> I Corinthians 12:4–5; 7; 12; 18 NLT

2

Remember: You Are a Diamond . . . Not Cubic Zirconia!

Too often, without provocation from me or prior knowledge of my journey or experiences, people—women and men—have said to me the following words or a close variation, "I know that there are women preachers because men have done a poor job in the pulpit. God *had to* call women to clean up the messes that men have made." This summation is an insult to both male and female clergy who have served and are serving faithfully.

Many men in the ministry have given of their time, talents, gifts, family, and personal resources. Of course, women in ministry have done the same. In my case as a child, if it had not been for men in the preaching ministry, I would not have had any examples of faithful, dedicated Christian ministry in that office. Later in life, when I served as program director for Sustaining Pastoral Excellence (SPE)—a Lilly Endowment grant awarded to Memphis Theological Seminary (MTS), I learned much from colleague groups who met monthly for 3 years. These groups were made up of 7–10 women and men who were clergy serving in various diverse ministry contexts. In the seven year period of the grant's existence, the groups discovered and confirmed, as I had suspected, that there was more commonality in clergy journeys than many had earlier surmised. There were life patterns common to most clergypersons. However, it was discovered that there were dissimilar and unique concerns or burdens placed on and experienced by female clergy, which had not been brought to the attention or awareness of most group ministers. Sometimes female clergy leaders were unaware that there were other women experiencing similar yet unique injustices and problems. Collegial support was welcomed by all but especially by minorities including female clergy.

Clergypersons—without regard to denomination, gender and race—grapple and struggle with similar issues and concerns. The beauty is that all of us can sparkle and shine *or* we can allow ourselves to become cloudy, dull, and chipped as we give service to our faith communities. As we move forward on the journeys of the kingdom, God would have us remain faithful but also to respect and realize the luster of other clergy who are having similar and different joys and injustices.

The calling of female clergy is not a result of the devaluation of male clergy. Women were created equal to men and were used and are being used in equal ways. There is no celebration or healthy collaboration that occurs while *putting down* women or men clergy. We can learn much from each other and help each other to discover our total beauty as we find ways to share common knowledge and to exchange unique narratives that will bring solutions to bear as we *all* seek to do faithful ministry.

Women who believe that they are substitutes for failing men then place themselves in a subservient or superior position with questionable usefulness in the kingdom! No woman's calling should be based on the commitment or lack of commitment of other persons—male or female. To say that God's divine call is totally dependent upon the action, reaction, activity, or inactivity of others is an insult to God. God created and called us with a purpose in mind. I believe that God equipped women and men with a set of gifts that will be potentially used to carry out our overall purposes. We can choose whether we want to fulfill our purpose. It is the job of every person to support the growth of all human beings as they seek to live out their calls and purposes.

Even though society in biblical days was traditionally focused toward patriarchy, it appears that in Jesus' earthy ministry he tended toward a more mutual respect of women in ministry. A personal favorite snapshot of men and women working together with Jesus is found in the gospel of Luke. It reads:

> *Soon afterward Jesus began a tour of the nearby towns and villages, preaching and announcing the Good News about the Kingdom of God. He took his twelve disciples with him, along with some women he had healed and from whom he had cast out evil spirits. Among them were Mary Magdalene, from whom he had cast out seven demons; Joanna, the wife of Chuza, Herod's business manager; Susanna; and many others who were contributing their own resources to support Jesus and his disciples.*

Luke 8: 1–3 NLT

While a beautiful and brilliant synthetic gemstone, cubic zirconia is a diamond simulant. Women preachers are not substitutes or simulants. They are rare and real. Authentic diamond quality is assigned by God and gradually uncovered and discovered as we all—women and men—live out our faith stories.

3

Sparkle As You Share the Load!

THE FATE OF MOST women is intricately connected to caretaking, supporting, and nurturing the lives of others. There are infinite examples from which we can draw. It may be a commitment to pets that require nurturing, neutering, bathing, feeding, or walking. It may be a connection to kids who are chauffeured to practices, dates, meetings, part-time jobs, or dental appointments. It may be a neighborhood nursing home network that leads to her volunteering to cut the yard, prune the roses, or feed the residents. Women have food on their plates that includes extra side dishes which are filled with the sweets, needs, and sadness of loved one. Before we give ourselves permission to let go of or reduce the duties that the web of relationships demands—if we are not careful— *we will often lay aside for too many years* the burden or opportunity of public ministry.

Often women postpone their own lives as they attend to the lives of others who may be intentionally or unintentionally demanding. It is not uncommon for male spouses to succeed at the expense of dutiful female mates. Often women have wasted youthful time before turning hearts toward discerning personal callings. When I accepted my clergy ministry calling I had to accept the reality that God was able to take care of my children, husband and my aging parents who were dealing with illnesses. While I clearly loved all the above people, I was shocked to discover that God loved all of them infinitely more than I did and God was their able primary caretaker! Even today in my 60's, I have to make a conscious decision to relinquish control of the care of loved ones to

God. Female ministers will have more difficulty submitting in this manner but it *must be done* as they fulfill their calling.

I discovered that my assignment was to give service to whomever God requested. We would all do well to trust the Divine as the Holy Spirit leads each of us to a perfect plan for serving others—one that will require sacrifices but not total self-depletion. Our God does not ask us to give to the point of poor self-care and lack of balance. The Eternal does not require us to give to loved ones without some aid and assistance—solicited and otherwise. Women can learn to ask for help when needed and to determine when it is time to allow others to share in responsibilities for the care of others including those who are very young, disabled, or elderly. Female clergy must learn to solicit and permit parishioners to fulfill their callings so that the church body can serve in harmony and cooperation.

The gospels and Hebrew Scriptures give us the pattern for living—to love God with our entire self and our neighbor *as we love ourselves*. The average woman—lay or clergy—must be reminded that godly love of self is equal to love of neighbor. At the same time and as much as we love neighbors, we must love and care for ourselves. Self needs underwear as much as babies need diapers!

As quoted from Deuteronomy 6: 5 and Leviticus 19:18, Luke 10: 27 NLT reads:

> . . . *You must love the Lord your God with all your heart, all your soul, all your strength, and all your mind. And, 'Love your neighbor as yourself'.*

Conversely, if we are to let ourselves live out our faith as ordained or licensed clergy, we will also be blessed to remember *not* to follow after an often common male model that could lead us to a life of church work and community service that excludes family life and leisure. We are *not called to forget* how to play, to go on vacations, to attend non-work related gatherings or to engage in healthy conversations with mates, friends, and families. Any preacher must realize *and* act out his or her love and appreciation for personal loved ones as they do public ministry.

And as we minister to people, women will need to find a favorite place where they can look into their own eyes with the mind of God guiding their gazes. No church work or community service comes before the call to become an authentic Woman of God who seeks to be true to a flow of the fruit of the Spirit as exhibited in "love, joy, peace, patience, kindness, goodness, faithfulness, gentleness, and self-control." (Galatians 5: 22–23NCV) The fruit of the Spirit is more important than any title, accomplishment, degree, ministry, or recognition. Internal development and spiritual formation are keys to a private life that is close to the Spirit who gives peace, contentment, and health as we live and labor.

In the late 1980s after overworking with multiple responsibilities in a mega church ministry, I became anemic, unable to breathe freely due to sinus/allergy problems, and troubled with repeated aches (head, back and stomach). After living the work of that ministry, leaving their service, and becoming healthier, I received clarity in at least one area. I learned that if I was to last long-term as clergy, I had to rest and work intermittently and regularly. As I moved forward through later ministry contexts, I also learned that as I wisely worked, rested and reflected appropriately, others then had the opportunity to give of their time, talents and gifts. *There is one Savior and I was not and am not the one!* God is able to handle God's ministries and our families as we fulfill our purposes and allow others to fulfill theirs. As long as I hold onto the truth of the above diamond discovery, I sparkle more each day.

4

Disperse Light To and For All

They all ate as much as they wanted, and afterward, the disciples picked up twelve baskets of leftovers. About 5,000 men were fed that day, *in addition to all the women and children! Matt 14: 20–21 NLT*

They all ate as much as they wanted. Afterward, the disciples picked up seven large baskets of leftover food. There were 4000 men who were fed that day, *in addition to all the women and children. Matt 15: 37–38 NLT (Italics mine both quotes)*

JESUS FED OVER *5000 or 4000 people* in the gospel passages recorded by the writer of Matthew. The male writers of the scriptures did not include even an estimated count of how many women or children were present to eat the personal feast prepared by Chef Jesus and served by his new diaconate and board of elders! There is no imagination that is wild enough to conceive of how this thirty-year old Jesus stretched a few fish and loaves to the point of having leftovers. Surprisingly, the miracle was half reported since there was no female count taken. For certain, the children included girls. Girls and women were not significant enough to be counted, even though they ate the food and heard the message preached by Jesus. Women, then and now, outnumber the men in any congregation but curiously they were not counted *then* and sometimes are not counted *now*.

Even though I had spent a lifetime of attending Sunday School and seminars at several churches, not one preacher or speaker lifted up or pointed out the fact that the women and children were not counted. My eyes and ears had been trained to read the scriptures from a patriarchal approach. Thank God for the men and women who had taught me as a child, however, they discarded or disregarded words that I needed to hear because the understanding, esteem, and respect for myself and others needed to grow to capacity.

Even baskets of leftover food were counted that day but women were not. Women count. As a young woman and new preacher, I needed the Creator of All to disperse light on this familiar scripture. The phrase, "not counting women and children" were words that devalued or ignored half of the service area that day. People need to be included in the message of Jesus Christ so that they can be certain of the Savior's love for them and respect for their point of view.

I was a seminarian before I noticed the last few words of the passage of scripture. Two of my male professors—Dr. Steve Parrish and Dr. Paul Brown—had the wisdom and took the care to lead me to this passage with a fresh outlook that included the female perspective. For this illumination, I am grateful to Memphis Theological Seminary and also I am especially thankful for the friendship of three Baptists mentors—Dr. James L. Netters, Dr. Reuben Henry Green and Rev. Lois Moore Williams. With the patient help of others, I began to see in the bible *and* in everyday life an even greater presence of women in ministry. When I became a member of the Christian Church (Disciples of Christ) denomination, I finally fully embraced the ordination of women.

As we are educated and re-educated, I believe we have a responsibility to teach others in the broader community the truths that we have learned. And we can serve those truths to people in a loving, kind, and responsible way—careful not to chip their faith or destroy their spiritual beauty. People should know that there is a female presence in scripture and it was put there by the Creator of our faith. Girls should know that it is fine to shine and glow in the intense brilliance that God intended.

Often women are afraid to accept the truth of their calling and the calling of other female clergy. I have learned and am learning that accepting my own brilliance helps me to accept more easily the brilliance of other women and men. Clergypersons who happen to be female bring a fresh cut to the scene—one that is needed by the whole faith community.

As we bring to the attention of our congregations that women and children in the above story were not counted in the same way as men, then we encourage present day believers to not make the same erroneous exclusions. For the good of all . . . women, boys and *girls too* should be appreciated, valued, and counted as we do ministry and show love to ourselves and others. There are some little girls who need permission to develop into the women preachers that God intended. As the church faithfully reveals and accepts the presence of women in ministry, there are some little boys who need our help as they learn to respect, affirm, and even champion women who choose to pursue their calling to preach and to lead God's people.

The Holy Spirit is waiting to be able to disperse gifts of preaching and proclamation to some young woman who needs the confirmation that women preachers and pastors are welcome to the feast of the faithful. Now and in the future, our work is to remove blindness and barriers to our own service flow and the service of others.

5

Dare to Mine the Minds
Where the Lord Directs

I AM A PERSON who learns best when I see an example of what has to be done. When I was a young woman I was an amateur seamstress who could make curtains, bedspreads and cute dresses for my two daughters. I did good work when I purchased and followed fabric store patterns but I did the *best work* when I patterned myself after my mother. As a young girl, I had seen my mother cut out patterns, put in zippers, or make button holes . . . As a young adult, sweet childhood memories were with me as I sewed articles. During early marriage years, I had my memories and one girlfriend who was a sewing partner as we created beautiful pieces for our children and our bedrooms. Patterns and partners for living out a *faith calling* are granted by the Holy Teacher of us all.

When I was completely confused about how to be a preacher, the Great Spirit sent me holy sample pieces to begin to help me shape my own life story. Rev. Lois Moore Williams was a woman who could look beautiful and stylish while preaching, teaching, and touching parishioners during healing services. I could see God's glow in her hair and hands. I could hear God's melody in her voice as she preached from her well-worn bible. I could sense God's presence as she lay soothing smooth hands on my head and chest. She showed authority when she prayed and she simultaneously showed respect and kindness toward her husband who was also Baptist clergy. In a land that was traditionally unreceptive to women preachers, she ministered with grace and power—later becoming the pastor of her own church. I was amazed at her ministry and it helped me to see what might be my future. Although her path did not include seminary, she was and is an avid bible student and teacher. My journey was different. God allowed and called me to attend two seminaries—Memphis Theological where I received a Master of Divinity and later United Theological that granted me a Doctor of Ministry. But I had to meet my first female clergy personal friend and mentor so that I could follow my formation path. God knew that I needed to see what I could become. My example was not my identical twin but she was my mentoring sister-of-the-faith. For Pastor Lois' example, I am and shall be eternally grateful to her and the Mother Eagle God. Dr. James L. Netters introduced the two of us in the early 1980s.

Dr. Netters, an African American Baptist pastor, helped me to see that God's gifts are broad and infinite. Clergypersons need education—both classroom and practical—as is reflected in his ministry to a large church located in a changing community that has many justice concerns. As this pastor led his church to become relevant and active he also became one of the first three African American Memphians to serve as a Memphis City Councilman. I saw him serve not only as a pastor but a political and civic figure moving freely throughout diverse socio-economic and multi-racial settings.

While serving as an associate minister with Dr. Alvin O'Neal Jackson, I learned to accept and ride the swelling and sometimes raging tides of parish ministry change when I saw up close a Christian Church (Disciples of Christ) church grow phenomenally and quickly. Due primarily to dynamic preaching, a strong radio and music ministry, and also innovative youth programming, that local church body rose from a membership of 500 to 4000 during my three year tenure. (After my leaving that ministry, the membership exceeded well over 8000 people who had their names on the roll.) Staff worked perpetually and faithfully as they pressed their way toward sustaining at least 60 active church ministry groups. Staff burn-out—especially clergy—was inevitable and common. While it was a highly celebrative and an extremely creative atmosphere, it was also very challenging. In that ministry, I learned how to recruit and organize a large congregational volunteer base and a multi-tiered staff. I did this while struggling to maintain personal self-care, sanity, spirituality, and family life!

One United Methodist (UMC) pastor, Rev. Bill Gaddie, showed me how to work in a ministry as pastor to a church in multi-layered transition. Rev. Gaddie, a white pastor, had served for 44 years in churches that were thriving and growing but he ended his pastorate working with a small church made up of people who were cautiously embracing a future that included a neighborhood which was transforming from a predominantly white population to a predominantly black one. As the full sanctuary that had seated over 1500 white people was replaced by the use of a chapel area that held about 200 white and black parishioners, Rev. Gaddie gave passionate and compassionate leadership to a transitioning and adapting church. He was a powerful pastor and a particularly gifted preacher who was insightful enough to lead parish committees toward reformation and acceptance of change. As a young Disciples of Christ licensed minister *on loan* to work as part-time staff at a UMC church, I arrived near the end of the congregation's transitioning process. I was enlightened and encouraged as I learned from a different denomination and this innovative, flexible pastor. Bill Gaddie also taught me the importance of doing some form of foreign mission work as a vital part of parish worldwide responsibility. Even as he served the church and the world, Rev. Gaddie was also a good father to his grown children and a loving husband to his wife with whom I still share camaraderie. His wife, Rev. Gail Gaddie, later went on to become a faithful UMC pastor. I learned more from Bill Gaddie in a few years than I could have learned in many formally conducted classes. He taught me as a father-figure, friend, brother, mentor, and colleague. And he did all of the above with a healthy sense of humor and liberal laughter!

And Dr. Reuben Henry Green, who died after 40 years of working in a local church parish, taught me that a minister can also serve in the world of academia and still be unafraid to embrace his or her ethnicity and work in the community. As a bi-vocational pastor, he served as the Chaplain and Professor of Philosophy & Religion at LeMoyne-Owen College (a Historic Black College), and also a professor and the president of the Tennessee School of Religion. He was dedicated to educating ministers in the African American community even if they were not willing or able to attend fully accredited institutions of higher learning. His studies led him to read Greek and Hebrew and to gather a vast library of over 4000 books on varied subjects including race, religion, literature, church polity, history, and children's ministry. Each Sunday, in his children's message, he told the story of one influential historical or present-day African or African American leader. Children and adults learned about their heritage from their pastor who was a dynamic preacher and friend. He believed in, embraced, and championed the cause of ordination of women preachers even when he was ridiculed by many of his Baptist ministry colleagues. As he walked 2 miles daily, he taught me the value of physical exercise for ministers.

People who trained me during the 1980s and early 1990s were different, eclectic . . . multi-faceted gemstones for which I am grateful. As I developed, all of the above mentors encouraged me, listened to me for countless hours, laughed with me, and accepted me as I was. They helped me to be better as they either demonstrated greatness or offered pointers and/or critiques with regard to my preaching, teaching, or pastoral skills. We did not always agree with each other but we respected and learned from each other. How I value each of their friendships and the opportunities that they gave me as a young preacher who was learning and growing up at their feet!

Sometimes I learned from one-time watershed events like this one that happened to me in the late 1980s. I was invited to preach at a small rural church in Mississippi. When I arrived early Sunday, I was greeted by an older woman who was wearing a starched white dress and heavy blocked heeled shoes. She appeared to be a sturdy person as she walked me to the front row of the church, after ignoring my request to be led to the pastor's study. She proudly told me, "You speak from the floor—down here. Don't no woman go up on that pulpit . . . 'cept for to clean it. If you need any water, I'll bring it to you." This was my proper welcome that day.

Even though the pastor, upon arrival, invited me to sit with him—in the pulpit area—and my sermon was well received by the people, I left that church with a somewhat empty feeling. Haunting questions kept me from getting much sleep that night. Why were some women and men so afraid of women preachers? Why did some people not accept the reality that women could hear the voice of God and lead people as well as men of the faith? Even though I was licensed, I asked *again* . . . Were there *really* women clergypersons? Was I a little crazy?

On the morning after this troubling Sunday church incident, I had been scheduled for many months to go to a workshop where I met Rabbi Valerie Cohen. She was physically beautiful, very intelligent, and she sparkled spiritually as well. She was younger than I and had a husband and children. That day I learned from her that Reformed Judaism had been ordaining women as rabbis since 1972. And God made this move without my knowledge or the permission of the woman in the starched white dress!

God did not leave me confused or doubting. God gave me holy snapshots of those who had either *traveled on* or *stepped alongside* the path that I was called to follow. Sometimes one-time conversations with people, such as Rabbi Cohen, gave me what was needed to allow me to feel comfortable in my own skin, even with its peculiarities. Encounters—a day or a decade or two—led me to know that God made me woman preacher. Even with flaws, faults, and failures, I had a determined mind to be focused and faithful to my calling.

To my surprise, by the time I was 45 years old, I could glance back on a path that led me in this way. I was born into the National Baptist tradition, introduced by my grandmother to the Church of God in Christ charismatic movement, attended a Roman Catholic boarding school, worked for an Episcopal priest, joined the Christian Church (Disciples of Christ), served in a United Methodist congregation, and graduated from a Cumberland Presbyterian seminary! I was not confused but enriched and grateful for growth and religious diversity. This eclectic background helped me to easily go in and out of parish ministry and to shine as a prepared hospital and hospice chaplain who comfortably moved from one patient to another. God trained me in a unique way.

In 2001, Community of Faith Christian Church (DOC) elected me as their senior pastor. While serving this small congregation of approximately 150 people, I had the blessing of serving with four other ministers who were all at different levels of ministerial formation. Their gifts were diverse and their personalities blended to form a team—me, two women and two men—who cared for a church family who loved God. Although I had worked mostly in a mega-church setting, I was glad to *more closely* witness women and men in ministry working together to benefit the Kingdom. I found that living into the call of being lead pastor while living in female skin was uniquely more challenging. I often inwardly reflected and compared my journey to that of the men with whom I had served. I concluded that church people seem to sometimes criticize and scrutinize women far more closely and openly than men in ministry. For the most part, I and my church members loved each other deeply and they followed passionately. However, a small number of parishioners challenged my every move!

I learned afresh that *women and men do view ministry and life sometimes differently* but I truly enjoyed and benefitted from accepting each other's styles, ideas, and vantage points. The differences could sometimes become nerve-wracking but they primarily brought multiple levels of richness to the work. In some ways, I think that we mentored each other!

After serving as senior pastor to Community of Faith for just less than eight years, when I retired I left contented that I had served well on my watch even though I was unable to complete all that I wanted. I left local parish ministry in order to give full-time service to the Memphis Theological Seminary grant where I was a program director. I remained friends with those women and men clergypersons with whom I co-labored in parish ministry. At the time of this writing, one of them has planted his own Disciples of Christ congregation.

In 2011, I was invited by Dr. Frank Anthony Thomas to temporarily return to Mississippi Boulevard Christian Church in order to assist him in closing out his 15 year senior pastorate with that church. He had successfully built on the legacy left by Dr. Alvin O Jackson. For the first time in a mega-church, I saw a paid staff of clergy women and men who were working and serving in a reciprocal way as they ministered to a people who had been taught to value the equal, mutual ministry of women and men. It was also significant that there were some 10 or so clergy women who served in volunteer capacities alongside 15 or more male clergy who were serving in the ministry. It was a joy for me to witness this in my ministry and lifetime.

Many times women are called to positions in the church after a lifetime of working in jobs that are characterized as secular or part-time. Women should realize, as I did, that life-lessons learned at home, or while doing jobs for pay or without financial compensation, can be great training for work in ministries. Ministries can use the wisdom of mothers, volunteer leaders, organizational chairpersons, community activists, and others who have led people in a variety of settings. Before attending seminary, I had been a supervisor and training coordinator for the Tennessee Department of Human Services. All I learned from the field of social work was applied daily while serving in various ministry contexts. God is not wasteful.

I write this section to encourage and nudge women to accept their mentors, sponsors, and holy light-reflectors *whenever* and *wherever* they find them and God grants them. The God who promised to be with us always sends people in many packages. I am African American and so-called middle class but I have been enlightened by mentors and partners from different racial heritages, socio-economic backgrounds, denominations, and faith communities. I have received what I believe to be divinely appointed coaching from persons younger and older than I was at the time when I met them. I have learned from women and men of the faith who were seminarians, non-seminarians, clergy, and laity.

My growth came from fertilization and fraternization enjoyed with those in parish ministry, social work and health care related ministries. Further maturation came from absorbing ideas and traditions from several denominations and faith groups. God granted me the privilege of gathering collective wisdom from the joys, pain, and knowledge of colleagues who were diverse and different in their approaches and offerings. One cannot get all that is needed from one institution or one person. I learned that God shaped and formed me as I was allowed to *mine in the minds* of many mentors who gave me their time and support. These discovered jewels for my journey helped me to move in God's grace and to use God's gifts. I give this word of advice especially to female clergy. If God tells you to dig in a spot, dig deeply to the glory of God! See the precious gems that you find. Treasure the people you serve and those with whom you work. These stones will most likely be used in your future.

It takes a million or more years for a natural diamond to form in the earth's mantle. I am still in formation and I am yet learning from friends and colleagues. I believe this learning process ends at death. It was around 57AD when Paul wrote a letter to the church at Rome. It is believed that this was probably one of his last letters written before his death. That letter was delivered by a trusted female deacon, Phoebe. It mentions and addresses a diverse group of Paul's co-laborers. It reads,

> I recommend to you our sister Phoebe, who is a helper in the church in Cenchrea. I ask you to accept her in the Lord in the way God's people should. Help her with anything she needs, because she has helped me and many other people also.

> Give my greetings to Pricilla and Aquila who work together with me in Christ Jesus and who risked their own lives to save my life. I am thankful to them, and all the non-Jewish churches are thankful as well . . .

> Greetings to Mary, who worked very hard for you. Greetings to Andronicus and Junio, my relatives, who were in prison with me. They are very important apostles. They were believers in Christ before I was . . . Greetings to Tryphena and Tryphosa, women who work very hard for the Lord. Greetings to Rufus, who is a special person in the

Lord, and to his mother, who has been like a mother to me also . . . Greetings to Philologus and Julia, Nereus and his sister . . . Greet each other with a holy kiss . . .

Romans 16: 1–4; 6–7; 12–13; 15,16a NCV

6

Diamond Clarity and Sexuality

Three Narratives that Reveal Flaws

ONCE WHEN I WAS in a prayer circle, a man was holding my hand and his movements with his fingers were both disturbing and inappropriate. He never spoke to me during, before or after the particularly lengthy prayer. My husband and his wife were in the circle and neither of them was aware of the man's suggestive touches. The larger circle of more than 15–20 people had no knowledge of the occurrence or the infraction of my rights and invasion of my body space. This writing is the first time I have ever shared these moments with so many people. Being careful in the future, I never stood next to him at prayer time again.

* * *

A man asked me when I greeted him before a meeting, "Now what does that beautiful smile mean to me?" I wanted to say, "Nothing". I verbalized, "Good Morning!" My broad smile had no ulterior or deeper meaning. I had freely given it to 10 others before the meeting started. I was glad that the session was almost immediately called to order and there was no more time to discuss my smile.

* * *

And another time when I went to a woman's house for an agreed appointment in order to talk to her about her deceased relative, she came to the door with a see-through black negligee, stilettoes, and thong panties. She sat too close to me on her living room sofa as we chatted about funeral plans and she laid her head on my shoulder as she cried. I gently asked her to put on a robe so she asked me to leave her home. I would have thought it was my imagination or prudishness until the next day when she called to share her apology for her forwardness and inappropriate attire on my home visit. She asked my forgiveness which I promptly granted. She and I never spoke further about that visit and I never made follow-up bereavement visits to her home when I was alone.

* * *

Above are three examples of several tough spots that appeared while I was doing ministry. The Body of Christ –the church—and its friends are flawed. In nature, the most valuable diamonds have greater clarity because they are flawless. There are no flawless people.

If you are a female in ministry, you are going to endure some sexual harassment or at least some inappropriate sexual behavior that could happen in private or public. Boundaries will sometimes be tested at peculiarly strange times. Also it is natural for clergy themselves to have normal sexual desires and feelings. It is our choice how we will handle our own natural feelings, those of others, and possible problematic occurrences such as the ones stated above. With God's help, we can bring clarity to each situation as we live out our faith.

I believe that God wants us to follow the Holy Spirit's leading even in the midst of a changing, twisted world that will often point us to a different set of morally acceptable behaviors displayed in social media, popular television shows, and theatrical performances. We are to shine in a manner that pleases God and brings people closer to the Kingdom.

Society, the Church, and Sexual Conversations

In the United States of America, there are daily references to sexual activities or sexual intercourse. Television shows, commercials—even advertisements for milk, cars or peanut butter are chunked full of implicit or explicit references to sexuality. However the church is slow to mention the subject during Sunday morning or Wednesday night worship that most members do not attend. Sunday School classes and bible study materials are not quick to mention the one thing about which people are thinking, talking, or chatting on the Internet. And even with all of this constant communication and focus by a broad range of people of all races and socio-economic backgrounds, pastors and people do not talk freely about sexuality, sexual intercourse or sexual preferences. Even though men and women are having sexual relations freely, the church universal only discusses it rarely and shyly. When discussions are made, it is relegated to the "Thou shalt not or Do not" (Ex 20: 14; Eph 5:3) category! Seldom do we revisit the book of Genesis which demonstrates the beauty, holiness, and indeed the command to "be fruitful and multiply". (Gen 1:28) In the congregational setting, neither pastor nor people mention body parts by name. All of the above brings an undercurrent of tension or pseudo secrecy when the church refers to sexual matters.

Sexuality becomes a blatant matter when a female pastor becomes pregnant. With each day that her stomach shape changes and expands, the congregation must face the fact that their pastor is having sexual intercourse—or at least she had it once! If the female pastor has a husband, her husband is allowed to be proud but tasteful in his remarks. It seems to me that married women clergy are allowed to talk about or allude to personal sexual activity if the conversation is rare and not too explicit. If the female clergyperson is single and pregnant, some board decides if she will be retained or dismissed. *Double standards yet exist* and still can emerge in the form of complaints if the situation is just right.

In the modern media, sexual intercourse between single sexual partners is more commonplace and seemingly acceptable to the public than marital intimate relations. On a weeknight during primetime, large television audiences watched a popular television series that showed the fictitious president of the United States having or trying to have passionate sexual relations with a woman who was not his wife or so-called fiancé. In the storyline, the political leader seldom even hugged his spouse and the married couple's substantive conversations were primarily limited to political affairs and aspirations. After watching enough episodes, somehow these interactions became almost acceptable and *normal* to television audiences.

For decades, married couples in television and movies were shown in twin beds with blankets tightly tucked and stretched to protect the privacy and separation of bodies! Even now, scenes with married couples having sexual relations are scarce. The implications for the church and its teachings are complicated and conflicted. Society then seems to say that it is *more acceptable and indeed preferred* for single consenting adults to have sexual relations than it is for married committed couples to do the same.

This all being said, parishioners become uncomfortable when a female clergyperson shows signs that she is having sexual relations, even with her spouse. More so, if the female clergy says she is openly lesbian with a female partner, she is certainly a rare flower that grows in the church world. Due to strong prejudices and biases, lesbian women will more than likely face even greater challenges than their heterosexual sisters. I believe most local church bodies have some trouble imagining their staff minister having intimate relations with males or females in heterosexual or homosexual relationships. It may be more comfortable for the church body, (even though quite painful and sacrificial for the clergyperson), to imagine that their Protestant ordained or licensed church leader has taken vows of chastity like Catholic nuns and priests! After over forty years of marriage, I am personally grateful that it is not so.

Statement of the Tension

People have sexual needs, desires, and thoughts. Often female clergy can be the focus of people's attention and fantasies. It is natural to grab the attention of others as we speak and preach in public or as we lead in various capacities. Sometimes clergy can be perceived as being powerful and even sensual as we conduct liturgy or lead others in singing or praising. Music of the church often mimics romantic songs that are played on the radio or on our electronic devices. People listen to all types of music as they exercise, play, and pray. While sacred music is designed to point us to God, it also connects us to people in the pews or in our fellowship halls.

Some parishioners are drawn to the sensitivity and attentiveness that is shown by their pastors, counselors, chaplains, or clergypersons. As we show concern and compassion, clergy serving in so many capacities can be misunderstood or misinterpreted. On the other hand, preaching can be an exciting and electrifying experience that causes clergy to be seen in especially illuminating ways. In the congregational context, all of the showmanship, candles, drama, pageantry, and the use of sound equipment can create and amplify an aura of sensuality. I believe that some of that which was described above is God intended. I also dare to believe that often hairstyles, clothes, robes, and even make-up of women can be used by God as a drawing card to help clergypersons to tell their stories with passion and color! I humorously think that even nail polish, lipstick, and the way we walk can enhance our person, thereby lifting Our Savior so that some person or persons will be drawn to get closer to being part of the Kingdom of God. *Spirituality and sexuality can flow from all that we are and whatever we do.*

We are called to care for *self* as we care for neighbor. This care *of* and *for* self will sometimes be confused by others—especially those who are outside of the household of faith. As you move deeper into ministry, you *will* have people who will make passes, and offer opportunities to break marital vows and/or all commandments! As in the corporate world, there could be those persons to whom you will report who might possibly offer advancement opportunities for requested sexual favors. You might be tempted (even if briefly), by a handsome or beautiful older adolescent for whom you are responsible in your ministry context. Do not be surprised if a young adult may briefly turn your head or get your attention for a moment.

Since women are often even more nurturing than their male colleagues, people will sometimes more freely share with female clergy some of the most intimate details of their life stories. As a hospital chaplain, I repeatedly discovered and rediscovered this fact when medical doctors would tell me that patients whom they had successfully treated for 10 or more years would tell me facts in a half-hour chaplain's visit that they had never shared with their physician or previous male chaplains. Do not be alarmed if you become tempted or troubled by what you hear. You are human.

All that we have—body, mind, and spirit—should be used to bring attention to Our Lord. While God means it as a demonstration of God's glory and beauty, we clergy can intentionally use our bodies to bring *ourselves* fame. Men or women of-the-cloth who choose to do so, can use their God-given authority, charisma, personalities, and power to confuse, abuse, manipulate, or support people. To some extent, it is our choice. However, some of this is in the minds of the people.

Sexual thoughts and feelings can show up at the most odd times. While serving as an associate pastor, a wife had been to my office to tell me a long story about her husband of 20 years and his recent infidelity. Her solution was for me to call him in and confront him with the unfaithfulness. I, of course, asked her to confront or talk to him and then I suggested that they *both* return to me together so we could do some initial counseling and then decide on next steps in choosing a possible appropriate referral source. She agreed. In three days, after having a conversation with his wife, the husband returned to my office *alone*. He was tearful, said he was repentant and very open about his affair. He told me in gross detail about his affair including one scene where he described how he had disrobed the second lady and had sexual relations with her in her home when her husband was at work. He cried and pleaded as he told his story. By the time he had "confessed", I felt violated and aroused! I needed to return home to my own spouse in order to regain my composure and receive comforting release. If that same incident occurred today, I would have stopped him in the middle of his storytelling so that I could stay focused. I certainly would have at least guided him to share less explicit details so that we could agree upon a time for him and his wife to return together. I view this story as both humorous and revealing. Sexuality in the church is never simple.

Godly Feminine Sensuality

All clergy—male and female –can attract others. However the female shape, natural beauty, and society's media portrayals can somehow cause females to appear more charismatic, sensual or alluring. These are God-granted gifts that we should use with care and prayer. I believe that we should make every effort to look like God loves us and that the Holy Spirit trusts us with our bodies and spirits. Clothes that we wear should look like the Spirit was oper-ating when we purchased them. Hairstyles and shoes are special touches that should be hints that say "Yes, Jesus loves me"! Smells on our skin should be sweet smells that point to God. I believe that the kiss of God should be apparent as others see our skin and hair. I also believe that women should be glimpses of the Beauty of God's Spirit. While being mindful of boundaries and with the intention of right living, we should not shy away from this physical or sensual part of ourselves.

After listening to the stories of several women in various settings and at numerous stages in their lives, I have come to the following conclusion. Even though it will probably be very chal-lenging, if the female clergyperson identifies herself as lesbian, I believe she should appropriately be honest about her sexual ori-entation before taking a leadership position. Hiding only causes future problems. She and the ministry context will decide if they will be "open and affirming", quietly supportive, or if they will not support her sexual orientation. Truthfulness and honestly can eventually bring freedom and peace.

Advice on Being Sexually Faithful

The following are a few suggestions that I have found helpful in keeping myself within healthy boundaries while in ministry. The last section of this book lists several general overall practices that help clergy to remain faithful, balanced, and whole in body, mind, and spirit. The final chapter practices and what I list below are not only those things that I have embraced in my own life but the list has been developed from many chaplain's visits with clergy—especially females—who were doing life reflections as they prepared to transition from this life to the next. Hospice and hospital patients who happened to be female clergy taught me so much. Sustaining Pastoral Excellence female clergy also shared intimate nuggets of truth that I valued. Without revealing identities, I will share the following section which contains collective wisdom that is not always found in books. You are invited to choose what gives you the most support and encouragement as you live into becoming a female clergyperson who has a sense of wholeness and balance— especially with regard to sexual practices and your sexuality.

1. Have fun in your own skin and style.

   If you like high heels or flats, wear them. If you are more a tomboy or a ballerina, *be* that and *show* that as you wish. Be who you are unabashedly and unequivocally and let others decide if they will love you. It is their decision and it is your life to live. As William Shakespeare wrote in his play, *Hamlet,* "To thine own self be true." And as scripture reads, " . . . and the truth shall make you free." (John 8: 32)

2. Socialize, date and have some fun as you do ministry.

Jesus certainly did. He was invited and he went to feasts, weddings and gatherings regularly. Why he even put on a fish fry for his partners *after* the resurrection! (John 21: 12–13) We know that he laughed and smiled because the "common people heard him gladly" (Mk 12:37b KJV) and children relished his touch and presence (Mk 10: 13–16). I think that he healed people's spirits by the laying on of hands *and* his hugs. As he created the best wine at the Cana wedding feast, he must have had a swallow or two. (John 2:1–10) God likes a party. Angels throw a party when we get closer to the Kingdom of God. (Lk 15: 10)

People in our ministry contexts need to learn to play and relax. And they need to see us doing the same. Church dinners should do more than feed our bodies. People of all ages can be encouraged and uplifted as they learn to play together.

I have found that relaxing conversations with women and men keep me relevant, more well-adjusted, and in sync with society as I continue to grow into a whole person. Jesus kept women and men in his presence as they had mutual conversational exchanges.

Surely, we must be wise in choosing with whom and where we will socialize and have playtime. Everybody cannot be in our inner circle of close confidants. But without this social component in our lives, we will become imbalanced, overwhelmed and burdened. Ministry can bring joy and sadness. Friends and acquaintances help us to bear the loads and to keep a positive outlook as we do the work of Our Lord. *While giving attention to healthy boundaries, we need to cultivate, maintain and cherish male and female close acquaintances and friendships.*

3. Seek and accept the Holy Spirit's guidance and strength as you manage your sex life.

The bible tells us to have sexual intercourse after marriage. Certainly, intimacy of body, mind, and spirit keeps a married couple happier and healthier as they grow together. If one or both of the couple is a minister, satisfying touches between loving marital partners makes life-in-general and ministry easier and richer. However, with phones ringing, people requesting appointments, endless texts and mounting emails, it is a challenge to allow enough calm and peace so that sexual intimacy, energy, and romance are maintained and enjoyed! Married clergy have to be intentional about guarding and enjoying intimate spousal time.

Single adults are directed by God's word to refrain from sexual intercourse. In this, I am not certain of the practicality of this commandment in a world where people are living well into their 80's and 90's. If you are single, you and God must decide if you will remain an adult who has chosen celibacy as a way of life. *I do know this,* if you are going to be a minister of God's word, too many sexual partners or casual sex acts will affect your ability to think clearly and remain faithful in carrying out ministerial duties. An undisciplined sex life will confuse those *to* whom you give and *with* whom you do ministry. Remember mentees are watching, celebrating, and mimicking your behaviors as they continue to grow and make choices for their own lives.

Divine power and guidance are needed to manage healthy sex lives of both married and single individuals who are clergy. As you become more comfortable with touching and being touched, you will probably become more appealing and sensual. I invite you to let the Holy Spirit keep you in this natural growth.

Married and single female clergy are strongly encouraged to plan and live into healthy, wholesome, entertaining activities and events that are not necessarily ministry context related. You may prefer to do some enjoyable things alone.

Try new things. Keep your mind occupied. Go bowling or swimming. Join an exercise group. Try walking in the mall, sewing, gardening, cake decorating, painting (walls and portraits) . . . Watch a new television show or go to a movie that is different than your regular genre. Diversify and learn. Meet new people who may have fresher ideas. Explore another part of your brain! Do something that you always wanted to do but never took the time or had the nerve to do. Sermons will get even more relevant and richer. You will personally sparkle with freshness, sensuality and newness of life.

4. If any relationship or habit begins to feel inappropriate or outside of your belief system, tell God and a trusted friend or mentor so that you can explore options and remain faithful to your calling and commitment to Jesus Christ. Consider professional counseling as needed.

> As Jesus and the disciples continued on their way to Jerusalem, they came to a certain village where a woman named Martha welcomed them into her house. Her sister, Mary, sat at the Lord's feet listening to what he taught.

> Luke 10: 18–19 NLT

> When a woman who had lived a sinful life in that town learned that Jesus was eating at the Pharisee's house, she brought an alabaster jar of perfume and as she stood behind him at his feet weeping, she began to wet his feet with her tears. Then she wiped them with her hair, kissed them and poured perfume on them.

> Luke 7: 37–38 NIV

In Samaria, Jesus came to the town of Sychar, which is near the field Jacob gave to his son Joseph. Jacob's well was there. Jesus was tired from his long trip, so he sat down beside the well. It was about twelve o'clock noon. When a Samaritan woman came to the well to get some water, Jesus said to her, "Please give me a drink." . . . The woman said, "I am surprised that you ask me for a drink, since you are a Jewish man and I am a Samaritan woman." . . . Then the woman left her water jar and went back to the town. She said to the people, "Come see a man who told me everything I ever did. Do you think he might be the Christ? So the people left the town and went to see Jesus.

John 4: 5–9a; 28–30 NCV

7

Diamonds Are Found in Deposits.
Shine in Solidarity

YOU ARE NOT A diamond solitaire. The church of God does not allow it and God does not approve of total isolation or a hermit-like state for serving in the Body of Christ. Periods of solitary reflection bring solace and serenity that is needed for long-term work in the Kingdom. However isolation is not the way to get things done or to keep things going.

When I was a pastor it was easier to only focus on shepherding the people in my local church parish because there was always plenty to do. Every month, even in a small church of less than 150 people, there were those who needed hospital or elder care visits. Periodically, there were funerals of members and births of beautiful babies who needed blessing. From time-to-time, the married couples needed counseling. And the growing amount of single couples, living apart and together, wanted to talk about their growing concerns and sometimes their growing households. They wanted church resources and blessings without the privilege or burden of marriage.

In any local congregation, especially depending on the age and size of the congregation, it is expected that there will be dying and deaths—physical bodies, failed businesses, broken partnerships, troubled friendships, hard divorces, and melancholy seniors who are navigating the changing waters of life—at home or in the nursing home. In faith communities, all of the above *and much more* must be attended to . . . along with weekly preaching and on-going individual weekly pastoral care visits that could last for months before healing or referral time comes. *No pastor can fly solo.* Help is needed and should be desired. However, grooming co-laborers requires teaching, training, patience, meetings, listening, and a certain amount of appropriate trust. Laity *and* clergy have parts to play in order to fulfill the needs and mission of any ministry.

Other Local Church Clergy

Serving with other ministers can be anxiety provoking at times but most times I found it to be a joy and a comfort to share the load. I discovered a few good and wise things to remember.

- **Somebody else can preach besides you!** God speaks to the people around you and God wishes to use others to sometimes deliver messages of hope and love in a refreshing manner. When I was a senior pastor, God blessed me always with at least two other clergypersons who were periodically invited to preach—even at Sunday morning primetime! The people were accustomed to the fact that I would not preach for at least one Sunday a month. The scheduled time for the associate's preaching was rotated so that all ministers got maximum support and attendance. I learned to treasure those times of rest and renewal. Many times I was refueled for the ride and I received a germ-o-truth for the next few sermons or bible studies that I would preach or teach. I learned this from the people already named who mentored me. (I was invited to preach in many pulpits prior to becoming a senior pastor, then as a co-laboring associate pastor, and now I preach as a retired visiting preacher doing supply preaching. Preaching in fresh settings and listening to others preach keeps me fresh, ignited, and relevant.)

- **Some people who are called to be associate pastors can greatly enhance all that you are trying to accomplish.** We, in time, can confide in them and bounce ideas off of them as the ministry develops. Their gifts can often complement our own. It is not good to fear them or fight them, especially in public! God can bless senior, associate, and assistant ministers to work together to do the work of the Kingdom. We should do all possible to keep an open faucet of flowing communication, prayer, transparency, collegiality, respect, and love.

- **Know that friendships can be broken and can sometimes evolve but if God is in the midst, the victory will come in time.** Only those closest to you can bring the most sorrow. Eleven choices for friendships were good but there was one Judas Iscariot in the group who was less than faithful to Jesus when Jesus needed him most.

Once I had a minister, a deacon and a trustee who colluded to discredit me in public and to squash an idea that I had shared with them. Even after their honest opinions were solicited at a board meeting, they chose to remain silent and appeared to be in agreement. Those at that meeting could have openly and honestly discussed and probably resolved the matter. However, they chose to communicate on emails to each other and a larger audience. Copies were finally forwarded to me by church members who were not even a part of our leadership team! I unknowingly thought the matter was settled. We later communicated clearly and our plans were adjusted so that they became much better than before. We actually had a laugh about the whole occurrence.

After reflecting on the hurtful and humorous situation, I thought perhaps, I was so excited in my presentation; maybe I did not give them a chance to share their true thoughts and feelings. *Clergy in leadership have to be certain to let other leaders around us shine when they have ideas or input that will help the body.* When pastors allow other leaders to shine, there is always a chance that they will outshine you and they could possibly even lead others away from your leadership and what is believed to be your God-given focus. However, it is a chance that we must take in order to enjoy and experience the blessing of collaborative work in the Body of Christ. We must trust God to bring us all together into one faithful unit. In nature, diamonds are discovered in rich deposits. In jewelry, diamond clusters glisten beautifully in settings.

City-wide and Regional Clergy

If you are serving in a city, there is no way for you to do faithful ministry without supporting and sometimes working with other clergypersons who live in your city, county, or region. There are common issues, concerns, challenges, and moments of celebration that touch the larger community and neighborhood. These matters are broader than just your immediate area of service. If you are too detached or isolated to interact with others on these city-wide or regional concerns, both you and those whom you lead will become very one-dimensional, weak, and unaware. Not only sermons and lessons must speak clearly to community concerns but your presence on certain boards, councils, and at some rallies are a part of your call to ministry and your faithfulness to God and God's people. Justice cannot be accomplished in isolation.

Sometimes it is time to speak out with the community and to march forward in visible unity with other local and regional clergy. As was the case with me for years, even if you are a chaplain whose hours are spent inside an institution or work facility, it still is a part of ministry and civic responsibility for you to vote, to gather at press conferences with other clergypersons who have similar strong beliefs and/or to persuade others to do so. To give to causes outside of our local context is a part of our mission to the city-wide and regional community in which we are deposited.

Because we are often so overburdened with our own local ministry contexts, it may seem impossible to spread our energies to the point of involvement in outside concerns but the God of Justice calls us to get involved with some social action *as the Savior directs*. Sometimes women are so overwhelmed with individual, family, and local parish ministry that they are tempted to ignore the calls to do justice and to partner with other ministers from other denominations or faith communities other than Christian. I shudder to think what would have happened if clergypersons and clergy spouses such as Martin Luther King Jr. and Coretta Scott King had taken such isolated stances!

I am inspired by women of the bible such as Ruth who left her birth community of Moab to follow her mother-in-law, Naomi, who was a woman of God. Even though Ruth's husband was dead she still embraced and journeyed with her widowed mother-in-law saying these brave words that are often read at weddings, "Don't urge me to leave you or to turn back from you. Where you go I will go and where you stay I will stay. Your people will be my people and your God my God." (Ruth 1: 16. NIV) We forget that this *march-forward-saying* was spoken by a young widow to an elderly widow as they prepared to travel to a country not previously seen by Ruth. The pay-off was a future filled with a much larger territory allowed by God and a new husband for Ruth. However, Ruth commissioned herself before she knew about her bright future in Bethlehem. God honors a community that shows unity and solidarity in times of need.

Denominational and National Clergy

As a senior pastor and associate pastor, I almost had little to no contact with clergy who were serving in other cities or countries. This was a flaw in my ministry. At the time, I felt I was too busy or did not have the funds to participate in some denominational events and activities. There were times where my ministry context did not provide the necessary funds for my participation so I would have had to spend my own monies to not only transport myself but also to take care of my family's needs while I was out-of-town. Sometimes General Assembly larger denominational discussions seemed to be unrelated and trivial in comparison to the leaking water that was flowing in the church basement or the troubles and everyday lives of my teenage daughters who needed my listening ear and immediate care. I made personal choices that kept me closer to my family and the local church family. Often while serving in a mega church body I was the "Cinderella Associate Minister" who had to remain home with the flock to chair the meetings or preach while others flew around the country or the world. Sometimes I wonder if I should have taken more trips offered to me . . . even though I did serve faithfully with the local church.

My congregation and I *did* make sizeable and regular donations to worldwide, denominational and regional causes that focused on the needs of people who spanned the globe. Our charitable dollars went places that we did not go. Occasional sermons raised the consciousness of the members with regard to the marginalized and poor in our local and worldwide community. There was intentional and concerted focus, at least twice a year, on the needs of missions that gave service and care to homeless and battered women and children. The men in our church family visited those who were incarcerated and in recovery from alcohol and drug addiction.

I am cautioning clergy women to intentionally and selectively use opportunities to have conversations with those holding political power and clout. Without your voice in such conversational exchanges, you will be ignored when the time comes for some appointments, promotions and recognitions. If the denominational or political powers-that-be are not somewhat familiar with your face or have not heard some of your opinions, they will then be unaware of your personality, service given, commitment level, apparent gifts, talents, and abilities. On the other hand, male leaders must also realize that sometimes women (unless taught) are not automatically good at posturing or bragging. Female clergy are *not necessarily* those who will *blow up* membership counts or budgetary figures in order to inflate a story told to other clergy! Men should learn to simply listen to what women tell them and to directly ask women preachers for things that they want and need to know. Male clergy would do well to learn that the woman sitting next to him in a judicatory meeting may have a balanced budget and a congregation size that is triple his own but she may choose to spend her time talking about her two year-old child and the new household puppy! It is her choice. However women should know that if you do not verbally share some of your successes, you run the high risk of being ignored, devalued and dismissed. Without substantive conversations, men and women do not have the benefit of female clergy knowledge and wisdom. Many men may need to learn from women to chat casually and socially *and also* to have authentic professional exchanges. *Some women have to be taught and all women must choose to let their lights and accomplishments show so that others can see and appreciate their sparkle and clarity.*

Mentoring Other Clergy

This section is written in order to challenge and encourage female clergy to not only foster friendships for your own growth but you are encouraged to grow friendships that feed and mentor those who are faithfully following a path that is fresher or younger than your own. We are urged and compelled to serve as a mentor to those whom the Lord assigns us. Most of the time God has given me at least 1–2 people to whom I pour ideas, words of wisdom, or give occasionally words of caution as allowed. These colleagues have given me *more than* I have ever given to them. Conversations may only occur monthly or occasionally but they have also blessed me to grow and to remain relevant. For example, additional skills in technology were gained because younger mentees passed along tips that this senior citizen probably would not have acquired on her own! Fortunately, I have had the pleasure of mentoring and learning from both male and female clergypersons as we mutually enjoyed each other's company.

Sometimes we are to teach *men* to respect and value the presence and offerings of females. Sometimes we are to teach *women* how to better relate to the men in their professional and personal life. *Mentoring is a part of being a Woman Preacher.*

Periodically, we are called upon to mentor those who are younger in the faith or younger in ministry but older chronologically. The age of mentees does not matter as much as the stage of formation at which they find themselves. When I entered the preaching ministry, I was married and had two children who were under the age of 12. I had been successfully employed as an eligibility counselor, a state training coordinator and a church/civic volunteer. In several settings, I was a *grown-up* but as a fresh start seminarian, even though I was almost 40 years old, I was scared, insecure, child-like and somewhat confused. I greatly wanted to have a mentor. Sometimes people need mentoring until they find out how to function in their new life situation. One of the things that I love about being a member of the Christian Church (Disciples of Christ) denomination is that the process of licensure and ordination of clergy includes having a sponsor who is more experienced in serving as a minister.

Some of my best seminary students have been those who were second and third career students who were daring to follow new paths with the help of God. Those needing mentors come in all shapes and sizes with rich backgrounds and wonderful real life stories that can enrich the mentor as they both learn. In my opinion, two students who were Vietnam-veterans-turned-clergy gave me more than I could ever give them! Even though they did not know each other, were different races, came from different denominational backgrounds, and were in two different seminary classes, I found that their perspectives were rich, sensitive, earthy, and consciousness-raising. They *did battle* for the Lord in the classes where they were members. I was honored by them saying that my classes were relevant, practical, and spoke in a special way to their particular needs. For this I am grateful to the Divine Teacher.

I urge those who are seasoned in the ministry to mentor and encourage those who are chronologically younger and also those who are accepting their calling perhaps later in life. Give back to the clergy community when and where God directs and requests. You will be immensely blessed and enriched. Let the Lord lead you in how to do this. Believe that you have much to offer. There are an infinite number of unique ways to mentor others who are searching for understanding and encouragement. See a few examples of ways to mentor and support:

- Periodically teach a seminary class or church/community workshop. When doing so, I learn almost as much as the students! They help me to sparkle even after 25+ years of service.
- Help with doctoral student projects and papers.

- Make a monthly phone call or keep a lunch appointment with those younger in ministry.

- Share relevant handouts and emails.

- Send a quick meaningful text or use Facebook appropriately.

- Write a handwritten note of encouragement or send an electronic card.

- Occasionally give a donation to the ministry or family of struggling mentees.

- Serve on a board or two if the cause is meaningful to you.

- Reach out to women *and* men who show an interest and eagerness in hearing some of your stories. *Don't bore others but don't store up your stories either!* Others who are younger in the ministry may be blessed by wisdom and an *exchange of stories.* Listen with your mind and heart. Their shared stories may freshen up your own and even suggest wider applications than you had earlier realized.

Friends

One Christmas someone gave me a sterling silver angel that appears to be dancing and flying or floating. She now lives on my living room coffee table. While she is truly beautiful, the small inscription on her garment located below the left wing brings me the most joy. It reads, "Sisters are angels that lift us to our feet when we have trouble remembering how to fly." I do not know the author but I owe them a debt of gratitude as I do my girlfriends who have helped to bring me through some trying times such as the deaths of my parents or the fires that ripped through my home and later the church where I was the pastor. These friends were the people who floated nearby when I needed them most.

While I surely appreciate female friends who have stuck with me for years, I also treasure the friendships of male friends. Their male perspectives on personal and professional matters have proven to be enormously valuable and have saved me from making some unnecessary mistakes.

All of my friends have listened to my complaints, ideas, woes, and celebrations. Friends are gifts from the Holy Spirit. We cannot always habitually fly alone and still expect to fulfill ministry opportunities. Everybody needs friends and companions to lighten the load, overcome the challenges, minimize the pains, and to share the joys. All healthy people need to cultivate a few friendships.

If you are single female clergy, you are allowed and encouraged to date and to dance! *If Jesus, his buddies, and his holy mother could go to a feast and have a drop of the finest bubbling wine, why can't you?* (John 2: 1–11) Everyone is simply not worthy of being in your personal space or of being your close friend. If their character or focus is not in sync with the word of God, they are probably not an enhancement to your ministry or to your personal spirit.

Family

You and God will decide who your true family is; it may *possibly* be those connected to you by genes, vows, and bloodlines! However, it could be God-granted family who will give their hearts and resources to minister to you and support your dreams, person and ministry. Guard family but do not worship them. Conversely, do not disrespect or ignore them.

Married Female Clergy and Spouses

If you are married, your spouse deserves a smile, hug, conversation and playtime—in and out of bed. The only one who has vowed before witnesses to remain in your space for a lifetime is your spouse. If only for that "death do us part" promise, clergy spouses deserve love, respect, and care. My husband has supported me even when I could not figure out how to support myself. Solomon has sacrificed time, money, and energy to me, the ministries that I have served, and to our children and grandchildren whom he loves. He loves God through Jesus Christ and has a personal relationship with Our Lord.

Being a clergy spouse is not for the faint-hearted! As a Sustaining Pastoral Excellence Program Director, I had many group and individual conversations and feedback sessions with clergy spouses. Those 40+ men (including my husband) and women taught me that it was both a challenge and privilege to be called clergy spouse. Some parishioners show love and respect while others pour out jealousy and envy to the pastor's wife. Because of lower congregational preconceived expectations, male clergy spouses often seem to have a better fate than females but sadly sometimes *all* clergy spouses are ignored or devalued as the membership pours praise and respect on the pastor. Clergy spouses are too often forgotten in some ministry context settings and also on special occasions. I believe God calls spouses of clergy to a special place that should be respected. Clergy and people should show and voice gratitude as they say words of appreciation and give appropriate gifts to clergy spouses. As it is with other people of faith, *clergy spouses should have the freedom to be led by God as they make their own choices about where, when, and how to serve in faith communities.* They should be cherished and valued as any other diamond or precious gemstone in God's ring setting.

Single Female Clergy—a Family of One

I am compelled to write that if you find yourself as a family unit of one, you are personally complete and your household is complete. The Infinite and All-Knowing God creates families and lovingly deposits us into them. *A family of one is valid and whole.* Those who were apostles of Jesus and those who traveled with him were both single and married persons. I have found that often females can do a lot of fretting about finding a mate with which to take marriage vows. Sometimes it seems that female clergy can communicate and feel that God has left them to flounder if they are unmarried. This simply is untrue. Without a spouse living in your house, I urge you to please fulfill your ministry and follow your path as you preach the word of God to a dying world. Celebrate your singleness and wholeness. Treasure the friends, associates, acquaintances, colleagues and family members that God has granted and planted in your life story. Enjoy your privacy. Do not fill or crowd the rooms in your house unless God provides occupants of God's perfect choosing!

Should you decide to marry, let it be to a person who you see as a life partner who is sent by the Spirit of the Lord. I bring a word of caution. Any female clergyperson who attempts a marriage with a person who does not know and respect God is making a decision to have a short-term marriage and intense heartaches.

Children and Youth of Clergy

Children who are a part of clergy families are often teased, mildly mistreated, and unfairly held to impossible and unreasonable standards by the household of faith. The offspring of clergy or clergy couples are sometimes called *preachers' kids or PK's*. Unfortunately, the hair, dress, speech, friends, tattoos . . . of *preachers' kids* are criticized and scrutinized if the faith community does not approve or understand the child's choices. On the other hand, the pastor's child can be pampered to the point of spoiling or smothering so that the clergyperson's children are expected to get the lead in every choir solo or church play! In some settings if the child makes even the smallest mistake, overwhelming excuses are made on the child's behalf. For example, if the senior pastor's child says an Easter speech, the praise is so overwhelming that I have seen PK's expect this doting to continue throughout adulthood.

Ultimately, children and youth want to have healthy loving relationships with their parents. They want to be accepted and not badgered by their local church body. Youth need balance. Clergy families are happiest if they put time and energy into mutually enjoyable quality activities for children and adults. Individual *at-home preaching* to children, especially those in your family, is not meaningful and most of the time not helpful. I found that talking *with* and listening *to* children and youth is helpful, hopeful and far-reaching. Playing and praying together never stops. I still do both with my young adult daughters and their friends!

Parents—single and coupled—will need to schedule appropriate times apart from children so that they can rest and refuel. Talk and listen time is needed at all ages and life stages. Being a parent to the children and youth in your care is just as important as attending to the needs of the children of the ministry context where you serve.

Family Nurture

Give quality time and care to your birth family and the loved ones with whom you live. They are your earthly shelter from the storms that will come. Remember:

Your spouse needs as much attention as the Elder Board.

Your home nursery needs as many inviting colors and fresh designs as the church nursery walls.

Your blood sister needs a phone call as much as the church mommy group members.

And the youth group should not have more sex education and more life skills than the youth in your family.

Female Clergy! Get some personal help such as housekeepers, clerical assistants, live-in helpers, or part-time drivers where and when needed so that your family will not suffer for lack of attention and you will get some needed relaxation. Make yourself available to love and to be loved.

A diamond is usually found housed in Kimberlite rock which is found in volcanic pipelines or alluvial deposits that are about 90 miles under the earth's crust. *All Kimberlite rock does not contain diamonds.* For those rocks that do have diamonds, the precious gems were formed when temperatures of over 2200 degrees Fahrenheit and extreme pressure caused carbon atoms to crystalize. This entire diamond formation process could take several thousand years. Kimberlite rock rests inside of volcanic pipes and may be unearthed during volcanic eruptions or perhaps when erosion causes rainfall or snow-melt to wash diamond-bearing rocks to the earth's surface. *All volcanic pipes do not have diamonds.* It is Creator God's choice which rocks and pipes yield diamonds. Natural diamond deposits contain groups or clusters of gemstones other than diamonds. *Diamonds are rare* and they are usually discovered by miners who are skilled and patient at removing, uncovering, and examining enormous quantities of rocks and other materials.

I liken the above tedious and lengthy process to the occurrence and formation of a good preacher and especially a woman who accepts and pursues her calling while often being challenged by a resistant society. It is a lifetime of adventure and discovery. With the process, God sends companions and loved ones to lighten the load and point to the best paths. I believe that all people are deposited into our lives with purposes and according to our Maker's plan. Women Clergy, where are your friends, family and associates in your life? Are you mining for them? They too are precious discoveries.

Surrounding yourself with other diamonds and precious stones can only make you look even better. Diamonds in jewelry look best when they are displayed in a cluster of other diamonds—in a setting that points to the main stone. In the spiritual sense, the Main Stone on display should be Jesus Christ Son of the Living God.

> *Standing near the cross were Jesus' mother, and his mother's sister, Mary (the wife of Clopas), and Mary Magdalene. When Jesus saw his mother standing there beside the disciple he loved, he said to her, "Dear woman, here is your son." And he said to this disciple, "Here is your mother." And from then on this disciple took her into his home.*
>
> John 19: 25–27 NLT

> *At dawn Jesus was standing on the beach, but the disciples couldn't see who he was. He called out, "Children, have you caught any fish?" "No", they replied.*

Then he said, "Throw out your net on the right-hand side of the boat and you'll get some!" So they did, and they couldn't haul in the net because there were so many fish in it . . .

Then the disciple Jesus loved said to Peter, "It's the Lord!" . . .

"Bring some of the fish you've just caught," Jesus said . . .

"Now come and have some breakfast!" Jesus said . . . Then Jesus served them the bread and fish. This was the third time Jesus had appeared to his disciples since he had been raised from the dead.

After breakfast Jesus asked Simon Peter, "Simon son of John, do you love me more than these?" "Yes Lord", Peter replied, "you know I love you."

"Then feed my lambs", Jesus told him . . .

John 21: 4–7a; 10a; 12a; 13–15 NLT

In the same way, you should be a light for other people. Live so that they will see the good things you do and will praise your Father in heaven . . .

Matt 5: 16 NCV

8

Diamonds are Hard—Not Brittle!
Guard Against Bitterness

EXPECT IT. THERE WILL be more than a few people who are close to you *and* outside of your personal sphere who will cause you sorrow with regard to your ministry. It was so in my case. Your job, my sister clergy, is not to allow yourself to become bitter or brittle!

I have found that people fall into at least three categories that do *not* support women clergy.

- There are those who do not believe that there is the entity of clergypersons who are female gender. (This category does not refer to those who doubt the existence of a divine deity. Such people have no need of a mouthpiece or messenger from a perceived non-entity!) This category covers those who believe in God but they have no room in their theology or belief system for female representatives of that Divine Entity.

- The second category includes those who *do* believe in female *and* male ministers but they do not believe that a *particular* female is assigned to do the work of ministry. Usually there is some sin or several sins that preclude the particular woman from being included in the clergy count. Also, the woman could have some missing credential that males have been required or requested to obtain. If the female in question is without the piece-of-paper or oral examination, the questioning parishioners feel justified in withholding approval of the woman's ministry. Oddly, males who announce their callings are often immediately accepted and supported until they obtain missing credentials. On the other hand, sometimes women have almost impeccable character and multiple degrees related to ministry but their characters and credentials are often ignored, devalued, or minimized by laity and, at times, other clergy. Male clergy may or may not be held to the same stringent requirements as their female counterparts.

- The third category covers those who *appear to approve* of female clergy. However, they show their approval *only if* the female minister is *not holding a senior leadership position*. To further amplify this third category, it is my experience that many times those persons who show the greatest disapproval of female clergy in leadership are those who have been elected or appointed to serve in other congregational offices. Perhaps their strong differing moral or political beliefs are such that they find themselves at odds with clergy in leadership. Perhaps they think that their power is threatened. In the eyes of many church members, laity power, clout, gifts, and position are threatened when clergy authority enters the room. Some people feel that they must *defer* to the office of clergy while others think that they must *fight* the office of clergy! Either stance is not good and breeds a contentious and suspicious atmosphere for all.

  If the senior pastor happens to be female, sometimes the disagreements turn into what appears to be gender related battles since the lay or other clergy leadership positions are often held by males. Gender biases which focus on the female tendency to view life more relationally and the male tendency toward a more success-related viewpoint, may sometimes collide to start long-term battles that can chip away at congregational and individual peace.

  I found it to be personally curious and hurtful when persons who had supported me as an associate pastor suddenly withdrew their support or friendship when I became their senior pastor. Certainly men go through some of the same kinds of challenges that were recounted above but it seems to be more frequently suffered by women. I am also not oblivious to the fact that when one assumes the lead position in any organization or an organism such as the church, the new leader sees things from a broader vantage point. It was certainly so for me. My wider and deeper viewpoint caused me to change some pervious stances and ways of handling matters. This change caused disappointment and feelings of betrayal by a few people who had certain expectations that could not be met after the leadership office was assumed. Any leader—man or woman—is stunned by the changes in alliances and reactions of people in whom they had built trust prior to assuming the leadership position. Because women are usually more relationally motivated, the cut or bruise appears to be deeper when friends or acquaintances withdraw or withhold support.

Whether persons do not believe that women can represent the Divine One or whether they do not believe in a particular female being called to serve as clergy, or if they are fighting female clergy because of their top leadership position or differing viewpoints, styles and vision—the opposition is real, loud, clear, and seemingly never-ending in some cases. *Each category is a form of rejection* and it can bring hurt and harm to female ministers. However, on a greater level, I believe that large amounts of valuable resources are lost from the Body of Christ when women are not allowed to use their gifts in the manner in which they believe that they were assigned by the Holy Spirit. Whatever the reason, the aggravation with fighting these battles is the stuff that causes clergy to lose sleep, get wrinkles, and it can start a pattern of multiple health problems. If clergypersons are not careful and prayerful, it can cause them to leave assignments prior to their completion and to sometimes be rendered almost ineffective. I do not believe that this has to be so and that the damage can be minimized.

The following are *three narratives* that will illustrate a portion of what is stated above and describes some of my own personal frustration and story.

Narrative # 1

In my life as female clergy, I have periodically suffered tension-related backaches, breathing problems, panic attacks, loneliness, rashes, confusion, and doubts although people tell me I have a totally calm and happy exterior. Humorously and seriously, one of the main sources of struggle has been about what to wear for any given event! This is a unique challenge to women in general but a particular problem for women-of-the cloth. Do I dress in a robe or no robe? Do I wear a dress, skirt, slacks, or jeans while in and out of the pulpit area? Should my attire be long, short, mid-calf or knee length? Do I agree to drape those hideously large, lace handkerchiefs over my knees when sitting? Should my make-up be soft or bold? Should my hair be cropped short or allowed to grow long? Shall I paint my nails or leave them bare? Will I tempt some-body by what I wear or do not wear? Is *anything* too tight? Are my clothes fitting too loosely so that I look frumpy and fat? Should this woman preacher wear sandals with heels or no heels? Will my toes distract from my delivery of the Word of God? *Do I care? Does God care?* Should I struggle to cover the beautiful breasts and legs that God gave me because men are struggling with their own con-sciences and sexual fantasies? Will there be 10 people who will not respect or reject women preachers because of what I say, do, and choose to wear? Is the outfit that I chose to wear outdated so that others will think that I am not relevant and up-to-date? These are some of the haunting and daunting thoughts of women preachers who are finding their ways and who are preparing to lead people in the pews, on the streets, on the battle fields, in the prisons, and in the hospital beds of the world. It is not fair but female clergy are forced to regularly wrestle with the above questions. Too often, women get a double dose of pressure poured out on them because of closer scrutiny. This layer of truth adds to the frustration and weightiness of serving as female clergy and it is only one example of many unique stressors.

One lady clothed in all black with long sleeves and thick stockings said to me on a hot southern summer day, "Baby, you are always welcome to come back to this church. We love you . . . but when you come back here—cover up those arms, like the rest of the saints!" . . . Later, after my eyes watered, I never returned to that church.

Narrative #2

Once when I had been a senior pastor for over three years or so, I had to do battle with a church treasurer because of a philosophical and theological disagreement. Our small congregation had voted and then made a practice of giving one-tenth of our collected tithes back to the community through charitable gifts to worthy organizations or other church ministries. Many times this practice could be a little unsettling but as long we were faithful to this commitment of giving, our budget was balanced and our bills were paid. As we wrote the checks to others, we might *seem to be low* in funds but we never ran out of money.

The treasurer understandably was cautiously concerned but her concern grew to a point of rallying support and calling a special congregational meeting to discuss our giving practices and the hiring of needed clerical staff. The treasurer thought that the church's fiscal stability was threatened. . . . Before I knew what was happening, we were at a meeting with two women in power suits—I in royal bluish purple and she in silver taupe! People were lined up on both sides and ready to do battle. Even some folks who had not recently been attending worship services came to the meeting on that day. We looked like military personnel. If we had worn brass or badges, the scene would have been complete. I won the battle but I do not know if I won the war. We then re-hired the clerical staff and the practice of donating the monthly charitable gifts continued. The treasurer ended up leaving the church and I lost her treasured friendship. I still believe that the course we took was a good one but the casualties of this church war were traumatic—internally and externally . . . individually and collectively.

The above story is one in which both leaders happened to be female. . . . One could easily say that this story could happen with men being one or both of the leaders. Even though the church had overwhelmingly voted to make the agreed upon charitable donations and although the church budget was still balanced, the unique element in the story is this. It was repeatedly said that *because I was a female pastor, I had lost my logical reasoning*. It was said, publically and privately, by some members that I was overly compassionate and was weakly leading the church in the dangerous direction of unsound financial practices that would quickly deplete church resources. . . . It seemed to me that when there was a point of contention, often my point-of-view was blamed on my so-called *female perspective*.

Parishioners have been challenging clergy for centuries. However, there *does* seem to be a societal imbalance that results in exclusively blaming the *feminine perspective* for decision-making rather than assuming that the female pastor and people may be having a simple difference of opinion. It does not seem that male pastors are accused of poor judgment *solely due* to their being male or having a male outlook. Conversely, is there a need for a softer more compassionate approach to some problems in ministry? Is the balance in perspective a good thing? I think so.

Clergy serving in other contexts suffer similar conflicts and tension. For example, institutional tenseness between hospital chaplains and hospital administrators can be hairy and insulting. While serving as a hospital chaplain and doing work that I loved with patients, I learned much about politics between institutions and clergypersons. After a series of meetings between the pastoral care department and hospital administration at a Level One trauma center facility, I suddenly realized that the hospital was not church! In a hospital, serving physically sick people was more important than chapel services or even dedicating a family room. Then curiously, a hospital business meeting *trumped* ministry to even the actively dying. Talking and listening to hospital staff was far less important than punching time clocks or writing timely entries in log books. I learned the harsh reality that auditors and insurance companies were little gods to whom all staff had to pay homage. Relationships did *not* supersede hospital quotas for required daily visits. I believe that these lessons are harder for women to accept because usually we are more relationally focused. After those meetings, I quietly began to execute my plan to leave hospital ministry and to find a more relational and (for me) a more spiritual path toward serving hospice patients and their families. Sometimes, women have to adapt or move about in various contexts in order to remain faithful to God's calling and to attend to our own personal formation.

Additionally, I have noticed in my life and it has been documented that male and female verbal communication styles are very different thereby fostering disconnections in understanding each other. Several times I could say something in a meeting—parish or hospital—that could not be heard until a male colleague said the same thing! Somehow different voice tones or perhaps different word choices helped the ideas to be communicated more clearly by the men in meetings. I feel certain that I know how to communicate since even my undergraduate work was spent in the fields of journalism, speech, and drama. There is something in the male voice and/or the patriarchal focus of our society that helps people to hear the voices of men more easily. All of the above can result in internal female frustration and confusion. After some hospital and church meetings, I left with my stomach in knots and my head pounding—just from feeling unheard or disrespected. As an African American female, I have had to learn to deal with what appeared to be racism, classism and gender bias when communicating in meetings.

Narrative #3

When serving as the Program Director for a Memphis Theological Seminary Lilly Endowment, Inc. Sustaining Pastoral Excellence (SPE) grant, the 100 program participants (who met in small groups of 7–10 for at least 3years) were made up of just less than one-half women clergy. African American and Caucasian men and women from at least 9 different denominations met monthly to transparently share stories and to encourage one another. From these SPE stories and from my own observations over the years, it seems that women clergy are often led or forced to accept positions that can be more dangerous or less glamorous. Sometimes we are given churches that nobody wants. Unfortunately, females are serving in congregations that have fewer funds so naturally financial squabbles and disagreements can become more frequent and intense. I have heard so many stories that I do not care to repeat. Women are often given the dregs and create something from nothing. Churches without working restrooms, with floors that creek or squeak, with broken stained-glass windows, and sour conflicted relationships are accepted by women who painstakingly turned those places of worship into little palaces with paying, hugging parishioners. When the mess is cleaned up, the water is mopped up and the mission is reformed, the better—new and improved building and local church body is presented to a young male clergyperson with a new baby and wife.

I have witnessed and experienced churches selectively buying into the myth of scarcity. As long as a female pastor is at-the-helm, there are people who say that there is no money for incremental raises or paid assistance—office or janitorial. I personally have cleaned church bathrooms during the week, vacuumed Fellowship Hall floors, and then preached on Sunday morning! However, as in my case after a voluntary retirement, when the male *interim* pastor arrived, he received greater benefits, a larger volunteer base, and a salary that doubled mine after my years of service that exceeded seven years. And I am certain that those people and I loved each other dearly!

In some cases, women may not put forth their best efforts when negotiating salaries. I think that I was somewhat remiss in this area since the mission of the church has always been a personal priority that superseded any discussions of salary. That being said, I have a strong suspicion that salaries of female clergy are often determined by factors that are unrelated to the merits and workload of the preacher or pastor. In my case, it was openly discussed and comments were made in my presence that since I had a husband with a good salary, then my church salary and benefits package could be more modest! I am not certain that this same salary and benefits *rule* would be applied to male pastoral counterparts. Even though grateful for my husband's salary and commitment, I found such comments to be invasive, insulting and unjust. At the time, I folded and pressed myself while choosing not to state my feelings. Even during this writing, I almost failed to mention this perceived unfairness.

Admittedly, female clergy will sometimes not demand or request assistance until becoming devoid of energy, patience, and financial resources. Speaking up and out assertively and repeatedly *might* correct some ills long before they grow out-of-hand. A healthy balance is not easily achieved but we must seek to remain self-aware, appropriately vocal, and prayerful as we negotiate benefits and compensation. We must teach people to give us gift baskets *and* checks.

Guarding Against Bitterness

I am grateful unto God that none of the above thoughts, stories, and questions *come* or *came* close to the joys of preaching, teaching, and sharing in ministry with God's people as they come closer to Christ's cross. Looking back, I would do it all again for the satisfaction and contentment of following God's calling on my life. In my case, for every ache or pain there have been infinitely many more laughs, giggles, and chuckles. So many parishioners and friends have sent encouraging, supportive thank you notes, cards, and flowers. I have received phone calls, emails, texts, meals, invitations to lunches, just when I needed them most. Church celebration days were sweet when I heard children speak simple yet sincere words of kindness and gratitude.

There were times in my ministry that I became fearful and had negative thinking that followed me around for many days. I had and sometimes now have sadness within myself –thinking that I may not be fulfilling my assignment but I never remain in that dim place for long. Many times, I entered the rainbow light after another person of faith cheered me on to a fresh space. I still love the church.

I want to emphasize that there have been many more church members and leaders who have given me loyal support, respect, and affection than I probably ever deserved! *However the negative and hurtful did exist and some of it was unwarranted.* I hasten to emphasize that I doubly appreciated church leaders who truthfully, lovingly, and faithfully cautioned me if they felt my course was incorrect or flawed. They were emissaries from God who added more wisdom to a thick pot of thoughts that were simmering or about to boil over! I love and remember the candid critiques and the encouraging words given in love and with respectful compassion.

The whole clergy trip was worth it when a grown young barely recognizable man bent down in the grocery store aisle to give me a kiss on the cheek while reciting with a deep voice and broad smile, his line from the children's Christmas play that was held so long ago. He continued, "Don't you recognize me, Pastor? Thanks for baptizing me when I was a kid. Meet my son and wife . . ." If we continue to lean toward making Spirit-infused choices, no bitterness can live in the midst of such love.

Over the past 30 years of ministry in several contexts, certainly, there have been times that I have received fair and more-than-adequate compensation for my labors in the ministry. There have been some preaching and speaking engagements at which I have received a few dollars plus some change and others which helped me to pay my taxes *and* the winter utility bill! I welcomed all honorariums and treasured even more the hugs and encouraging words that were issued with the money. When people tell me that their lives were positively changed due to the message that I preached or taught, the gratification is overwhelming. I praise God for the opportunity to use my gifts and skills. Tension and testing never exceeded the spaces and places of sparkle and shine. While serving God's people, we do not have to become bitter, broken or brittle. We can remain engaged and positive if we move forward in grace. We can choose to be strong, resilient, and flexible with the help of God.

For a span of 7 years and two grants, I learned from the stories and reflections of over 100 Sustaining Pastoral Excellence (SPE) clergypersons who met in groups of 7–10. As their SPE Program Director, I had the privilege of supporting and learning from the Colleague Group Leaders who met monthly with each other and with their assigned small clergy groups. We heard and noted the patterns and practices of those men and women who remained faithful and those who dared to stay most calm as they gave pastoral ministry. The following is a list of things gathered from those SPE leaders and they are also practices that I try to consistently keep in my own life. These are at least *9 things I have found that will keep clergy fresh, aware and connected with God and neighbors while encouraging internal peace and physical health.* Numbers 8 and 9 in the list below have words that are intended to be especially *unique* to women clergy. I believe that the things listed will help us to guard against becoming brittle or bitter when living out our clergy calling.

1. **Pray, mediate and read scripture daily that is *unrelated* to sermon preparation or other clergy duties.** I have found that even one day without doing this will result in nervousness, insecurity, less sense of well-being, excessive sadness, tendency to argue, and increased internal struggles.

2. **Have a few close friends including some clergy.** Habitual isolation is unhealthy. Find ways to connect with trustworthy Godly colleagues, associates, and friends. Use any means to find a few people to talk to about your personal and professional celebrations and challenges. Allow somebody chosen by the Spirit to enter your space so that you can be mutually accountable and supportive. *God does grant friendships.* Set dates on your calendar and keep them!

3. **Attend to your physical health**—even though it is not convenient. Eat right, drink water, get some exercise, and get enough sleep for your unique body's needs. Keep regular appointments with physicians appropriate to your age and life stage. Dare to follow their instructions!

4. **Plan and *do* regular rest and relaxation—at least once a day, week, month and year!** Play. One 15 minute daily break will not ruin your ministry effort! Remember if you go on a *so-called vacation or sabbatical* and then spend the time preaching, teaching, meeting, and consulting you have only changed work venue. No rest has occurred. I do not think that Jesus "got in the boat and went to the other side" in order to conduct a conference in another county.

5. **Connect and reconnect with God-given *family*.** If we will accept the gift, I have seen it that our God of Love always gives us a close circle of intimate people—blood relatives or otherwise—with whom to relate, share, and laugh. Sometimes in the life of being a clergyperson, one's blood family members understand us the least. It was so with Jesus. That being said, it is very important that we make every effort to share precious quality time with our spouses, children, siblings, partners and close loved ones as we do things that *mutually* matter to all involved. We must nurture and nourish *family* and allow them, in their own way, to do the same for us. Even though he usually wins, a game of Uno played with my 7- year- old grandson, Davie, gives me a treasured memory, many laughs, and helps me to grow!

6. **Give some attention to your financial health—present and future.** Too much focus on this area will cause anxiety but too little focus on it will cause the same or worse! Secure help, as needed, in planning for the future. *Follow the plan* and do *not be shy about asking ministry context officials to do their part* in maintaining clergy financial health and security. Make financial plans for your retirement and end-of-life expenses. Include discussions and plans with congregational leaders about matters such as disability benefits, life insurance, a pension plan, and reasonable incremental church co-pays. Plan for paid vacations and sabbaticals. As you continue to serve, revisit and update such discussions and plans periodically.

7. **Attend to your mental and emotional health.** Consider keeping a therapist, spiritual director, and/or attending a support group, as needed. Admit it and get help if you are overtaken by any addiction. (While publically living out their faith and helping others daily, too often clergy are closet alcoholics, chronic overeaters, and flirting with inappropriate relationships . . .) Confront others when needed. Forgive. Read and explore some positive books and internet offerings. Ask yourself periodically if you are pursuing some of your own dreams and aspirations. Make technology your friend but *not* your constant companion or master. Turn off electronic devices when you eat a meal with family or intimate friends. Laugh. Get a life-giving hobby or a pet. Give and receive holy hugs!

8. **Periodically, try to attend various national, regional, and local judicatory events and activities.** General Assemblies, synods, presbytery events, congresses, convocations, and such, are certainly not my favorite places to be found. The politics of the local church are more than enough for my plate. However, I have found that *if women are to move forward*, stay aware, and bring fresh energy to the ministry being served, it is more than valuable to create friends and alliances with related male and female colleagues—especially those in one's present denomination. *It is wise to speak out—* assertively and *not* aggressively—and to vote appropriately at some such events like those listed earlier. Because they are unknown to the powers-that-be, often faithful women clergy are devalued and ignored when promotional opportunities present themselves. Being repeatedly overlooked can bring bitterness, resentfulness, discouragement, and sadness. We must do our part to keep this from happening.

9. **Let your wardrobe and outside appearance reflect who you are.** After diamonds are dislodged from the rough dark rock that houses them in the earth's crust, they are washed, greased, cut, shaped, polished, and mounted in gold or silver. After their processing, these refined gems are finally

displayed on the necks, arms, ears of people who are adorned by their beauty, color, and charm.

Woman Preacher! Find your own personal style and embrace it. *Love yourself.*

- Get some clothes, shoes, robes, rings . . . that are worthy of your calling. Use color appropriately, tastefully, and lavishly. Wear shoes and purses that are comfortable, functional, classic and yet stylish. (Tiny purses for the pulpit or hospital hallways are an animal all-their-own! Invest.)

- Go to stores that fit your budget. Find the pieces that fit the body type that was given to you by your Maker. Creator God made you to be an attractive drawing card for the Kingdom's purpose and plan. Do not fear your femininity but do not distract from God.

- Find a haircut and style that is comfortable for your position and one that will remain well-kempt as you dash to meetings, worship services, dinner dates, and never-ending emergencies occurring at hospitals and home bedsides.

- Learn how to wear makeup as carefully and sparingly as possible but with colors and textures that will enhance and flatter your face.

- Use products that will thoroughly clean and soften your skin each day.

- Eat and drink appropriately . . . Lots of vegetables, fruits, fibers, and water will give you sparkle and clarity that no makeup can.

- Get regular exercise which will tone and uplift all body types and shapes.

- Give clothing items away if they no longer fit. Unless you have them for sentimental reasons, discard or do not wear pieces that are no longer in style. People will not tend to listen to or take seriously those ministers who seem to be non-relevant or out-of-step with present society.

- Wear eyeglasses and/or contacts that flatter and function properly for delivery of the Word of God and for reading in odd places such as graveyard services and dimly lit hospice rooms.

- Keep small healthy snacks, hand sanitizer, or wet wipes in your purse or pocket so that you can survive, remain patient, and be fresh until a sit-down meal break is available.

- Forgive, rejoice, and praise God! Unforgiveness, hatred, and unresolved anger create an unattractive aura and a generally unpleasant appearance.

Diamonds are the hardest natural substance known to humanity. They are basically a chain of carbon atoms that have crystalized to form the beautiful, valuable, durable, and rare stones that we enjoy in jewelry. Diamonds can be imitated but not duplicated. Through hot volcanic activity, extreme pressure and thousands of years, true diamonds are found deep inside the earth in an igneous rock known as kimberlite. Before the beauty of the precious gems is revealed, they must be mined, cut, and polished with diamond blades or laser. Creator God initiated the process in these stones *and* in the women that I know who have answered the call to become God's mouthpieces. The journey is not easy to yield the beauty that can come. If we remain faithful to the Spirit's path and do not allow bitterness to override love and peace, Women Preachers, we can have clarity and color that God can use to bless God's people and to bring us personal joy.

> *Then God said, Let us make human beings in our image and likeness. And let them rule over the fish in the sea and the birds in the sky, over the tame animals, over all the earth . . . So God created human beings in his image. In the image of God he created them. He created them male and female. God blessed them . . . God looked at everything he had made, and it was very good.*
>
> Gen 1: 26a, 27,28a, 31 NCV

Don't grieve God. Don't break his heart. His Holy Spirit, moving and breathing in you, is the most intimate part of your life, making you fit for himself. Don't take such a gift for granted.

Make a clean break with all cutting, backbiting, profane talk. Be gentle with one another, sensitive. Forgive one another as quickly and thoroughly as God in Christ forgave you.

Ephesians 4: 30–32 The MSG

And now, dear brothers and sisters, one final thing. Fix your thoughts on what is true, and honorable, and right, and pure, and lovely, and admirable. Think about things that are excellent and worthy of praise. Keep putting into practice all you learned and received from me—everything you heard from me and saw me [Paul] doing. Then the God of peace will be with you.

Philippians 4: 6–9 NLT

". . . fast for me . . . Then I will go to the king, though it is against the law; and if I perish, I perish."

On the third day [of the fast] Esther put on her royal robes and stood in the royal or inner court of the king's palace opposite his [throne room] . . . And when the king saw Esther the queen standing in the court, she obtained favor in his sight, and he held out to [her] the golden scepter that was in his hand. So Esther drew near and touched the tip of the scepter.

Esther 4: 16; 5: 1a, 2 AMP

Suggested Related Reading

Crawford, A. Elaine Brown. *Hope in the Holler: A Womanist Theology*. Louis-ville/London: Westminster John Knox Publishers, 2002.

DeRosia, Melissa L., Marianne J. Grano, Amy Morgan, and Amanda A. Riley. *The Girlfriends' Clergy Companion: Surviving and Thriving in Ministry*. Herndon: Alban Institute, 2011.

Epperly, Bruce. *A Center in the Cyclone: Twenty-first Century Clergy Self-Care*. Lanham: Rowman & Littlefield Publishing, 2014.

Jones, Kirk Byron. *Rest in the Storm: Self-Care Strategies for Clergy and Other Caregivers*. Valley Forge: Judson Press, 2001.

Oswald, Roy M. *Clergy Self-Care: Finding a Balance for Effective Ministry*. Washington, D.C.: Alban Institute, 1991.

Smalley, Gary, Greg Smalley and Michael Smalley. *Men's Relational Toolbox: Go Ahead. Open it Up*. Wheaton: Smalley Publishing Group (Tyndale House Publishers), 2003.

Smith, Christine A. *Beyond the Stained Glass Ceiling: Equipping and Encouraging Female Pastors*. Valley Forge: Judson Press, 2013.

Weinstein, Victoria. www.BeautyTipsforMinisters.com

Internet Website Offerings Regarding Diamond Formation and Mining

http://en.wikipedia.org/wiki/Diamond

http://www.ask.com/wik/Diamond?long=en

http://www.prevailmagazine.org/gods-diamond-in-the-rough/

http://www.madehow.com/Volume-2/Diamond.html

About the Author

COZETTE R. GARRETT IS an ordained Christian Church (Disciples of Christ) minister who is known as a lively and informative preacher, workshop leader, and speaker. She teaches and trains in a variety of settings while often focusing on the health and wholeness of God's people.

Dr. Garrett received an earned Doctor of Ministry from United Theological Seminary (UTS) at Dayton, Ohio, a Master of Divinity from Memphis Theological Seminary (MTS), and a Bachelor of Arts degree from University of Memphis.

Her recent past service as the Program Director of the Sustaining Pastoral Excellence Program—a MTS Lilly Endowment, Inc. grant—was quite fruitful as she had the privilege of supporting over 100 diverse clergy as they did faithful Christian ministry. She is a retired senior pastor who also served as both a trained hospital and hospice chaplain. Over the past twenty years, her work in church ministry has been broad as she served in both staff and volunteer positions at several churches including her present home church which is Mississippi Boulevard Christian Church (DOC). In order to pass along all she has learned she serves as a MTS adjunct professor of Pastoral Care.

Dr. "Coz" lives in Memphis Tennessee with her husband of over 40 years. They are the parents of two young adult daughters, Dana D. Garrett and Marloe Garrett Mackie. Marloe and Charlie W. Mackie are the parents of her wonderful grandchildren—Charlie David and Clarke Elizabeth Mackie!

http://www.cozettegarrett.com/